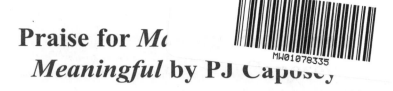

Praise for *Me* *Meaningful* by PJ Caposey

PJ Caposey has developed a great resource on teacher evaluation that actually provides realistic, encouraging, and supportive guidance instead of an arbitrary checklist!

—Larry Ferlazzo, Teacher, Author and
Education Week Teacher Advice Blogger
Luther Burbank High School
Sacramento, CA

PJ Caposey does it again! He writes with authority, relevance, and passion about a topic often researched and often avoided by practitioners. He shares tips and needed mindset shifts as well as concrete examples of how to maximize the inherent power in the evaluation process. He outlines how to take a process required by law into a meaningful and powerful learning journey for all involved. Caposey masterfully lays out a coherent structure for making evaluation meaningful and for equipping would-be evaluators with the "how" and "why" for conducting critical conversations. This compelling manuscript is a must-read for graduate students studying to become school leaders and practicing school leaders alike.

—Mike Lubelfeld and Nick Polyak, School Superintendents,
Authors of *The Unlearning Leader*
Co-moderators of #suptchat on Twitter
Deerfield, IL

Evaluation is an incredibly important and time-consuming responsibility for educational leaders. Caposey shares practical methods and notions that will move your evaluation process from good to great. Promoting the success of every student is directly tied to the type of feedback evaluators provide to teachers. Making Evaluation Meaningful *will change your mindset and push your school culture in a positive direction.*

—Brad Currie, Dean of Students and
Supervisor of Instruction
Chester School District
Chester, NJ

Quality feedback informs and provides practical suggestions for improvement and is pivotal if the goal is to improve teaching and learning. PJ Caposey, through a practitioner lens, has developed an incredible guide that not only helps to demystify the evaluation process, but also provide ready-to-use strategies to ensure reflection and growth are the result. In the end, evaluation must be meaningful for both parties. This book will help get you there.

—Eric Sheninger, Author/Consultant, Senior Fellow/Thought Leader
International Center for Leadership in Education
Cypress, TX

One of the most daunting and frustrating challenges for school leaders is making teacher evaluation count. Implementing a model is not enough. Through practical examples, PJ Caposey has discovered how to do the things school leaders want to do—build on strengths, develop shared meaning, and ultimately improve student learning. These goals are attainable with the principles shared in Making Evaluation Meaningful.

—David Geurin, Graduate Education Professor
Southwest Baptist University and Regent University
Bolivar, MO

PJ Caposey's book Making Evaluation Meaningful *is an important read for administrators and teacher evaluators as it addresses the overarching challenges with teacher evaluation, starting with the biggest issue in education, oversimplification. The book seeks to provide solutions that make evaluators more adept at providing teachers with better feedback to ultimately improve the learning culture in a school. Evaluation undoubtedly impacts culture, so the way we approach the process can and will have ripple effects.*

—Starr Sackstein, Author
Hacking Assessment: 10 Ways to Go Gradeless in a
Traditional Grades School; Blogging for Educators;
***Teaching Students to Self-Assess;* and many more**
Long Island, NY

For years, building leaders have been agonizing over teacher evaluations, pouring countless hours into a practice that consistently fails to produce the desired result: more meaningful conversations that produce improved quality instructional practices and increases in student achievement. In his book, Making Evaluation Meaningful, *PJ Caposey shares a step-by-step framework filled with quick and easy-to-follow "Tips for Tomorrow," as well as detailed examples to help you shift your mindset and become a more effective instructional leader. This book will leave you questioning your own evaluation system while at the same time inspiring you to re-commit the time and resources needed to help grow and develop your teachers.*

—Jimmy Casas, CEO
ConnectEDD, Inc.
Des Moines, IA

Dr. PJ Caposey is an award-winning practitioner and a leader on a mission. His continual pursuit to increase student and teacher success is also the foundation of his latest book, Making Evaluation Meaningful: Transforming the Conversation to Transform Schools. *Dr. Caposey delves into one of education's most sacred cows: teacher evaluation. He provides research, strategies, and insight into transitioning this often mundane and meaningless chore into a systematic process that is purposeful, reflective, and powerful.*

Right out of the gate, Dr. Caposey examines common evaluation practices, both good and bad, and provides a tool-kit of strategies to increase both teacher and administrator effectiveness throughout the evaluation process. He honestly recalls his own naivety and boldness in conducting evaluations early in his administrative career that resulted in fear and compliance. This book is a worthy guide, packed with practical and helpful strategies for both the evaluator and the evaluated, to establish an evaluation process that creates positive and effective protocols to strategically meet the learning needs of both students and staff.

—Julie Adams, NBCT
Author, Educational Consultant
Rocklin, CA

Making Evaluation Meaningful

Making Evaluation Meaningful

Transforming the Conversation to Transform Schools

PJ Caposey

Foreword by Todd Whitaker

FOR INFORMATION:

Corwin
A SAGE Company
2455 Teller Road
Thousand Oaks, California 91320
(800) 233-9936
www.corwin.com

SAGE Publications Ltd.
1 Oliver's Yard
55 City Road
London EC1Y 1SP
United Kingdom

SAGE Publications India Pvt. Ltd.
B 1/I 1 Mohan Cooperative Industrial Area
Mathura Road, New Delhi 110 044
India

SAGE Publications Asia-Pacific Pte. Ltd.
3 Church Street
#10-04 Samsung Hub
Singapore 049483

Executive Editor: Arnis Burvikovs
Senior Associate Editor: Desirée A. Bartlett
Editorial Assistant: Kaitlyn Irwin
Production Editor: Amy Schroller
Copy Editor: Karin Rathert
Typesetter: C&M Digitals (P) Ltd.
Proofreader: Alison Syring
Indexer: Jean Casalegno
Cover Designer: Candice Harman
Marketing Manager: Nicole Franks

Printed in the United States of America

ISBN 978-1-5063-7889-3

SUSTAINABLE FORESTRY INITIATIVE
Certified Chain of Custody
Promoting Sustainable Forestry
www.sfiprogram.org
SFI-01268
SFI label applies to text stock

17 18 19 20 21 10 9 8 7 6 5 4 3 2 1

Contents

Visit pjcaposey.com for additional resources to improve and transform schools.

Foreword

It is important that we support initiatives in schools that make a difference. It seems that often, this is not what happens with teacher evaluation. We place tremendous time, energy, and resources into doing something that we "know we should do," even if we can find little utility in the process. On top of the lost resources, we also add stress. This is not a winning combination, yet year after year we stumble through this process.

It is essential that we realize that people, not programs or policies, are what make schools great. We must inspire teachers and school leaders with strategies that help provide meaning to a job that can be overwhelming and stressful. In many ways, this is almost antithetical compared to much of the rhetoric surrounding teacher evaluation. That is precisely why this book is so exciting.

PJ Caposey has done an excellent job in understanding the human element of teacher evaluation. He demonstrates that he understands that no single framework or evaluation protocol is going to change a single teacher's behavior by itself, let alone an entire school. He moves from this paradigm and then examines every element of the evaluation process in an attempt to make it more practical, user-friendly, and most importantly, effective.

Making Evaluation Meaningful: Transforming the Conversation to Transform Schools is precisely what the educational community needs right now to continue to grow and change the conversation surrounding teacher evaluation. Teacher evaluation has been an exceptionally hot topic in schools for about a decade, and most districts have radically transformed their practices in order to meet the trend of the day. What has happened is little to no improvement in overall school outcomes and a ton of teacher and administrator stress. I love this book, because it can help decrease stress for all parties involved *and* it puts forth a plan where the evaluation process can actually help teachers grow.

There are two sections of the book that are particularly valuable—the discussion of the pre-conference and the improvement bank section. PJ does a great job of critiquing the pre-conference, by describing what many schools do but few people critically think through. It is discussed in detail with easy, tangible suggestions for improvement. Additionally, the back of the book contains a great compilation of improvement suggestions that can have real-world impact for many teachers. As PJ affirms, no administrator intentionally does a poor job in evaluation, but some lack the tools needed to provide meaningful feedback. The improvement bank section provides more than "some" tools—it is the Menards, Lowe's, or Home Depot of teacher evaluation, offering a plethora of resources.

This book is very exciting! PJ and I have worked together on multiple ventures, and I have always been a fan of his work, but this book is of particular value. Every chapter hits readers on multiple levels. It is philosophical and practical—it will change your paradigms and your everyday routine. PJ shares stories that many of you can relate to and he demystifies the cumbersome evaluation process into a series of smaller processes and systems, but most importantly, he never loses sight of the human nature of our schools and the evaluation process.

To paraphrase from my 2011 book, *What Great Teachers Do Differently*, any educator can study lists of guidelines, standards, principles, and theories. The difference between more effective educators and less effective colleagues is not what they know. It is what they do. The reason this book is so effective is that PJ does a great job of helping people understand what they need in order to *do* their job better. This is a practical, well-read, and potentially game-changing book when it comes to teacher evaluation. I trust you will enjoy it as much as I did.

—**Todd Whitaker**
Distinguished Adjunct Professor, PK12 Leadership
University of Missouri
Columbia, MO

Preface

Teacher evaluation has been a hot topic in education for over a decade. Increased emphasis on teacher performance originated from the era of accountability ushered in by No Child Left Behind. Since then, powerful and dynamic evaluation frameworks have been popularized, and a great deal of time, effort, and energy has been invested in transforming the once uneven and often routine process. After nearly a decade of effort and implementation to systematically improve evaluation processes in education, two things remain constant. First, achievement scores by nearly all measures have not significantly improved, and second, the overwhelming majority (95 plus percent) of teachers are found to be proficient or better in most states (Dynarski, 2016). This leads to the conclusion that current evaluation procedures are not fundamentally improving teacher performance. This book is intended to shine a new light on the evaluation process to help transform our practices as educators and ensure that the time spent in evaluating teachers is meaningful for both administrators and teachers.

WHY I WROTE THIS BOOK

I was once working with a district to revamp their evaluation procedures. On the second day of training, the chief administrators were called away, and I was left to work solely with the active practitioners. A principal, inspired to be more honest with the "bosses" out of the room, remarked, "I spend at least 80 hours per year evaluating teachers. How do I make sure that it is meaningful for both the teacher and for the school—because right now I am pretty sure it is not?" In that one short instance, I realized exactly why I was doing work centered on evaluation. Evaluation had become cumbersome, stressful, and time consuming, all while losing its apparent meaning to administrators and teachers alike.

In writing this book, I hope to do my part to help fix what ails the evaluation system. My experiences support and I truly believe that teacher evaluation when done well can systematically transform a school. My steadfast hope is that this book provides principals with the tools they need to make the process meaningful, comfortable, and streamlined. Additionally, I hope to demonstrate how, when done thoughtfully, the evaluation process can serve as the tie that binds all school improvement activities together.

With this book, I hope to provide the following for educators and the schools they serve:

- Improved teacher practice as they receive better support from their principals
- Improved student achievement because of better principal and teacher performance
- Clarity and purpose for administrators; making them more effective and their role easier
- Improved school culture as a result of clear evaluative expectations and protocols and with an increased focus on conversations to promote teacher growth

WHAT THIS BOOK IS NOT

This book is not a competitor to the established frameworks commonly used in schools. This is designed to be a tool that administrators can use to better implement the high-quality frameworks that are already in place. This book is not something you do once to fix a problem—it is a guide to transforming your school through a series of actions. More importantly, the focus of this book is to help teacher evaluators to rethink their role in the process and to help them critically analyze how they can adjust their practice to better serve their teachers and their school.

AUDIENCE

This book is written for teacher evaluators and those who are working hand in hand with teachers to help improve their practice on a daily basis. It is also my hope that superintendents and other district leaders read this as well. My experience informs me that teacher evaluators often feel isolated and rather unsupported. District leaders must too see themselves as instructional leaders who provide the resources and support necessary to construct a system that is meaningful and purposeful for all involved. It should be noted that the final few paragraphs of the concluding chapter are a direct plea to superintendents, with some logical next steps they can take to begin serving as leaders in this process.

GOALS FOR THE READER

Ultimately, I wrote this book to accomplish one primary goal—make the reader a better teacher evaluator. This can be accomplished by exploring the following, smaller, objectives:

- Help the reader understand the broad-reaching impact that teacher evaluation has upon student achievement, school culture, and sustained professional growth.
- Break down each element of the evaluation process in detail and help the reader to improve both through "quick fixes" and through cultivating a lasting mindset and paradigm shifts.
- Convince the reader that communication and confidence are key elements to being a great evaluator that truly supports and encourages teacher growth.

SPECIAL FEATURES

This book is designed to be user-friendly, by placing as many tools as possible in the hands of practitioners.

- Personal Experiences and Stories

  Personal experiences with districts and administrators drive this work, informed by research on best practices. Well-intentioned administrators who are struggling to make the evaluation process work for them will find that the stories resonate with their own experiences. The stories shared will help readers to personally connect with the content and help them understand that they are not alone in the struggle in trying to make evaluation meaningful.

- Tips for Tomorrow and Mindset Shifts

  Every chapter has a handful of Tips for Tomorrow, designed to be tools an evaluator can implement immediately. These smaller transitions toward positive practice help to keep the reader engaged and demonstrate easy ways in which incremental progress can be made. In contrast, Mindset Shifts are larger paradigm shifts. People often debate whether you can think your way into new behavior or if you have to behave your way into new ways of thinking. The combination of Tips for Tomorrow and Mindset Shifts appeal to both ideals and if employed, will lead to sustained change.

- Culture Assessment

  The connection between school culture and the evaluation process is often not readily apparent. When explored, however, the influence of evaluation and administration's role within the process have a significant impact upon the culture of a school building. Since this connection is not easy to see for some, this book contains a culture assessment focused largely on teacher evaluation. This tool will not only provide great insights for practitioners; for most, it will also create a sudden sense of urgency when they begin to look at both evaluation and culture through new lenses.

- CHANGES

  The book breaks down the seven ways a school leader can use evaluation to systematically transform the culture of their school. A playbook is given on how to leverage the evaluation process to positively influence the culture of a building so that it better serves the needs of both the adults and students within it.

- Suggestion for Improvement Bank

  At the conclusion of the book, a suggestion for improvement bank is provided. Often, administrators provide little to no feedback on how a teacher can improve their practice. As a result, the evaluation process becomes an assessment of value to the organization instead of a systematic process to help teachers grow. The reason for lack of suggestions for improvement is not evaluator effort as commonly believed—it is instead the perceived lack of valuable input to provide as an evaluator. As a result, sample suggestions for improvement are provided as an addendum at the end of the book.

- Dos and Don'ts for Teacher Self-Assessment

  Teacher self-assessment is a practice performed with different parameters in different ways throughout the United States and other countries. While the benefits of self-assessment are known, teacher evaluation can also bring forth anxiety for administrators. A simple dos and don'ts checklist provided in this book will allow administrators to have a strategic approach to teacher self-evaluation in order to capture all the benefits while mitigating the vast majority of the risks.

- Evaluator Self-Assessment

  One of the best features of this book from a practicality standpoint is an evaluator self-assessment that captures the three major phases of the process: pre-conference, observation conversation, and written document provided to the teacher. This not only serves as an assessment of practice, but also serves to help evaluators begin with the end in mind. A quick glance at the desired outcomes helps evaluators to remind themselves of what is truly important and to work to improve their own professional practice.

- Connections to Popular Frameworks and Best Practices

  While this book is not intended to compete with popular evaluation frameworks, it certainly acknowledges they exist and works to create clear connections between these tips to transform the conversation and the existing frameworks. Additionally, the book works to incorporate what we know as best practice through the work of Hattie (2012) and Marzano, Frontier, and Livingston (2011) to better guide evaluators in their attempt to use research to support their teachers.

- Online Resources

  Visit pjcaposey.com for additional resources to improve and transform schools.

Acknowledgments

I would first like to thank my wife, Jacquie, and our children, Jameson, Jackson, Caroline, and Anthony for continued support and encouragement. My greatest hope is that something I write someday benefits you or someone you care about.

I would also like to thank my Board of Education—John Smith, Kristine Youman, Tim Devries, Tim Flynn, Marsha Welden, Jill Huber, and Matt Rhodes. Your belief in me and willingness to provide me autonomy with accountability allows me to pursue all of my professional dreams. I cannot thank you enough for that opportunity.

Additionally, many thanks go to my Leadership Team, faculty, and staff at Meridian CUSD 223. I am beyond fortunate to walk alongside you and hope that I provide you one-tenth of the inspiration that you provide me.

Lastly, thank you to Tom Mahoney. Everyone should have a mentor and friend like Tom. He challenges me every time I speak with him and I grow as a result.

Publisher's Acknowledgments

Corwin gratefully acknowledges the contributions of the following reviewers:

Rich Hall, Director of
Elementary Education
Henrico County Public Schools
Henrico, VA

Dr. Louis Lim, Vice-Principal
Bayview Secondary School
Richmond Hill, Ontario

Beth Madison, Principal
Robert Gray Middle School
Portland, OR

Angela M. Mosley, Principal
Essex High School
Tappahannock, VA

Tanna Nicely, Principal
South Knoxville Elementary
Knoxville, TN

Kathy Rhodes, PK–3 Principal
Hinton Elementary
Hinton, IA

About the Author

 **PJ Caposey** has had a wide range of educational experiences throughout his career. Mr. Caposey's educational career began by receiving the Golden Apple Scholarship in high school, which supports students in pursuing their dream to teach by providing scholarship money and training in return for a commitment to teach in a need-based area. Mr. Caposey did just that after completing his studies at Eastern Illinois University by teaching at Percy Lavon Julian High School in the inner-city of Chicago.

After completing his administrative certification at National Louis University, Mr. Caposey served as an assistant principal in Rockford Public Schools before becoming the principal of Oregon High School at the age of 28. After arriving at Oregon High School, Mr. Caposey and the school received many honors. Personally, PJ was acknowledged by winning the Illinois Principal's Association/ Horace Mann Partners in Education Award and IPA Principal of the Year for NW Illinois. Additionally, Mr. Caposey personally has been selected as an Award of Merit winner by the Those Who Excel program sponsored by the Illinois State Board of Education, was honored as one of the nation's top young educators when announced as an Honoree for the ASCD Outstanding Young Educator Award, and has been named an ASCD Emerging Leader. PJ was named one of 25 superintendents to watch nationally by NSPRA and won the INSPRA Distinguished Service Award of Excellence in 2016 as well as being named to the 40 Leaders under 40 cohort in the NW part of Illinois. More important, Oregon High School was named one of the nation's top high schools by *US News and World Report* in 2012 and one of the top 2000 high schools in the country by *Newsweek* in 2013. Meridian has also been named a District of Distinction by *District Administration* magazine and is home to 1 of 20 schools in the nation named a School of Opportunity.

PJ recently earned his doctoral degree through Western Illinois University and continues to write and guest blog for many websites such as Huffington Post, Eye on Education, ASCD, Edutopia, My Town Tutors, and Test Soup. PJ has also penned two books—his most recent co-authored with Todd Whitaker—named *Building a Culture of Support: Strategies for School Leaders* and *Teach Smart: 11 Learner-Centered Strategies to Ensure Student Success*. In addition, Mr. Caposey also serves as an adjunct professor for Aurora University within their educational leadership department and a principal coach for the Illinois Principals' Association.

PJ is a sought-after presenter, consultant, and professional development provider and has spoken at many local, state, and national conferences. A short list of those entities which PJ has presented on behalf of include ASCD, Illinois Principal's Association, National Rural Educators Association, and AdvancEd. PJ also enjoys the opportunity to work in different consultative capacities for schools and other organizations.

PJ served as the Oregon High School principal for four years and currently is in his third year as the superintendent of Meridian 223. He is married to a teacher who works with gifted students and lives with his four children: two sons, Jameson and Jackson; and twin toddlers, Anthony and Caroline, in the Northwestern part of Illinois.

Introduction

"And it is those who start with the why, that have the ability to inspire those around them or find others who inspire them."

Simon Sinek

BEING AN EFFECTIVE INSTRUCTIONAL LEADER TAKES PRACTICE

I began the interview process for my first principalship at the age of twenty-seven. My experience at that point in my career was comprised of teaching inner-city Chicago teens and working as an assistant principal in (at that time) the second-largest urban district in the state of Illinois. I am not sure what made me think this experience had prepared me to be a rural high school principal—but I submitted an application anyway. Soon after, I was in the lobby of a district office preparing to interview in a medium-sized rural district in a town I had never stepped a foot in until the day of that interview. I was fortunate enough to progress through the interview process, then be offered and ultimately accept the position. I was young. I was confident. I had vision. I had no concept or understanding of how to lead a building.

I entered the position with two strong beliefs. Growing up in an authoritarian Italian American household and as an athlete, I believed in accountability and authority. I also believed in myself. I would have at that time stated proudly that I could out-work or out-read anybody. I thought technical skill, along with the willingness to get my hands dirty, would carry me to a successful career as a building administrator. I learned quickly the naivety of my ways.

My first year as principal was also the first year the Danielson evaluation framework would be used in my building. Let me be clear, this was not an innovation or forward-thinking move by me, this was just a coincidence of timing. Being me, I read and read and read every iota of material I could find related to the Danielson framework. I walked into that building exceptionally confident in my ability to use the tool effectively. My confidence was both warranted and idiotic. I should have been confident in my knowledge of the framework but not in my ability to implement it effectively.

As the school year began, I lived in teachers' classrooms. I believe, to this day, in the principal as instructional leader, and I was trying to live that adage out in my building. I collected evidence, gave frank feedback, and tied everything to the comprehensive evaluation framework that our district was implementing. In my head, I thought this would lead to the improvement of teacher practice, better service to kids, and the overall progress of a school with historically mediocre student achievement.

I was blind enough to move forward with my head down for months, but I was smart enough to listen to a few people who had the courage to pull me aside and tell me what I was actually doing to the building—to *my* building. I had created a culture of fear and compliance. I was not the instructional leader, I was the instructional dictator. The building felt icy and as if nobody wanted to be there; I knew for certain that I did not want to be there on most days.

LEARN FROM MISTAKES

I had choices to make and corrective action to take if I did not want to work in this type of environment. Fortunately, I had learned some things in those first four months, one of them being to talk to my faculty before making major decisions. With this in mind, I pulled a veteran teacher into my office one day after school to begin this conversation. This teacher always had the best interest of the school in mind and would tell me what I needed to hear, not simply what I wanted to hear. He told me it seemed as if I "was using the evaluation framework as a weapon." Wow! I immediately thought of the quote by Dr. Stephen Covey, "We judge ourselves based on our intentions and everyone else based on their behavior." While I in no way intended for teachers to feel this way, I realized no statement could have captured the evaluation practices in my school better. He continued, "Even the best teachers cannot find fault in the advice you are giving to improve practice—but this—whatever <u>this</u> is—has to stop."

Humbled, I sat in my office and tried to piece together the game plan moving forward. It literally took years to repair the damage I inflicted on the culture of the building, but eventually, we were able to move forward quite successfully as a team. From that point forward, I have been borderline obsessive about the role of evaluation in schools. As I continued to research, speak, present, and consult on the topic, trying to help others learn from my mistakes, I have realized the potential impact

> *"We judge ourselves based on our intentions and everyone else based on their behavior."*
> Dr. Stephen Covey (n.d.)

of transforming practice to make evaluation more meaningful. My mistakes were not isolated; in fact, poor practice surrounding evaluation is a pervasive issue in education. I believe that as educators we have an incredible opportunity to improve our evaluative practices and truly transform the conversation surrounding one of the more polarizing topics in education.

RETHINK ESTABLISHED THEORIES

Recently, I was at a friend's house for a get-together, and as the night progressed, one table outside quickly became the educators' table. As I looked around I noticed that I had not directly worked with any of the people involved in the conversation and eventually asked the question, "What do you see as the purpose of teacher evaluation, and why do we do it?" I followed up by asking for the "real" answer from them.

> "Accountability."
> "Because the state makes you guys."
> "To have a gotcha."
> "Keep tabs on the teachers."
> "To separate teachers—basically determine their value to the organization."

This string of answers came from a group of teachers I find to be generally positive and excited about their work in the profession. As I quietly sat back and did not say much, the conversation continued along these lines, until a few minutes later, a thirty-something male high school teacher said, "I guess the real purpose is to help teachers get better—it just does not feel that way the majority of the time." So I asked, "How many times have you had an evaluation that has been instrumental in improving your practice as a teacher?"

> "Two out of thirteen—both when I was younger."
> "Never."
> "Most of the time—but I have an amazing principal."
> "Every few years I will get a good idea or two."

Wow! Here is the sad part; I was not surprised by their answers. It was just shocking to hear them say the words. Again, let me reiterate—these are not negative teachers. These are teachers who by all accounts like their jobs, love their students, and care enough about teaching to talk about it with passion at a social gathering!

As I talked with each of my administrators, I asked, "How long does it take to complete an evaluation cycle—the pre-conference, the observation, the examination of data, the write-up, and the post-conference?" I told them I was not concerned with informal observations at this point—simply the nuts and bolts evaluation process. The consensus was between five and eight hours. My principals on average have approximately fifteen evaluation cycles to complete. In my experience working with principals in other districts, neither number (the time or the amount) is abnormal. That means, (very) conservatively, principals are spending seventy-five hours going through a process that most teachers find to provide little added value to them professionally! To look at this from another angle, principals are spending two full weeks of the school-year taking part in an activity that may simply be frustrating and stressful to every single individual involved without providing any added value to growth of teachers or education of kids.

> *If you examine the habits of highly successful people their schedule will almost maniacally match their priorities. #MakingEvalMeaningful*

If you examine the habits of highly successful people, their schedule maniacally matches their priorities. The priority is to use a systematic process to cause growth in teachers, so that they may better serve children. This creates a fantastic opportunity for improvement in schools, if we can shift the focus and improve our evaluative practices. This leaves us with the conundrum of having a time and stress intensive product that is not adding much value to our schools. The fact that administrators in schools across the country are spending time in teacher's classrooms and providing them feedback on performance is a profound step in the right direction compared to where we used to be. Simply put, the evaluation system in the overwhelming majority of schools and districts was a bit of a mess.

DON'T NEGLECT THE *WHY* AND *HOW*

While many instruments of this accord now exist, two have become the dominant force in teacher evaluation today: Charlotte Danielson's *Enhancing Professional Practice: A Framework for Teaching* (2011) and *Teacher Evaluation That Makes a Difference: A New Model for Teacher Growth and Student Achievement* by Robert Marzano and Michael D. Toth. Both of these documents and guiding set of standards for professional practice are legitimately wonderful. I mean this sincerely. I wish that I had such documents to build my practice around when I was still in the classroom. Additionally, they have helped to guide me as a support and coach to the practitioners I work with today. That said, these frameworks have not solved the issue of poor evaluation practices in schools. What is worse, they have not only been marginal at best in improving practice, they have been quite proficient in creating toxic cultures in many buildings.

The fundamental problem is that education, as an industry, attempted to address a very complex issue with a solution based on written frameworks. To use the concepts introduced brilliantly in Simon Sinek's TED Talk (2010), which is quoted to start the chapter—education started with the what and neglected the why and how. Think of it metaphorically—if you give a weekend golfer the best set of golf clubs in the world, they will likely perform better than they did previously. This does not make them great. In fact, this does not solve any of the fundamental issues that may have been negatively impacting their golf game for years. The new clubs are simply a better instrument with which to do a complex job. As a result, they will most likely lead to slight or marginal improvement. This is the same thing that occurred in the land of education with the introduction of the Marzano and Danielson frameworks. A better tool has been provided—but this tool by itself does not make an administrator a quality evaluator.

The recent intensive focus and research dedicated to teacher evaluation has created little meaningful change in our schools. In fact, many teachers would argue that the implementation of rigorous evaluation frameworks after years of lax and uneven evaluative practice has caused more segmentation among staff members and has added stress to the job. The story shared at the outset of this book about my personal experience is a perfect example of this.

FOCUS ON THE GOAL: IMPROVING PRACTICE

So approximately a decade or more into the comprehensive rubric/framework stage of teacher evaluation, it is clear this was not the silver bullet to improve teacher practice as people had seemingly hoped for. The silver bullet to teacher evaluation is extremely simple yet extraordinarily complex. The silver bullet is better performance by our people. The right people with the right mindset, training, and skills can turn teacher evaluation into a meaningful exercise that can transform practice. However, the question remains, do we value this change enough to make it a priority? If we do, we will build time, both as individuals and as institutions, to make our schedules reflect this priority. The best tool in the hands of an average evaluator will not make a difference, and the best leader independent of a tool can make a tremendous impact on the growth of teachers. As McKinsey (2007) said, the quality of an educational system simply cannot exceed the quality of the people within it.

The question this book thus tries to solve is, how do we improve our evaluators so that they can therefore help our teachers improve? Instructional frameworks set the stage for this change but are only one small piece of a complex puzzle. This book will attempt to give principals, other administrators, and superintendents a more definitive playbook on how to change what evaluation has become in our schools. Instead of a process that is entirely dependent upon the effectiveness of the evaluator and largely a waste of time, energy, and resources for the vast majority of educators, let's change this process into something that builds relationships, is looked forward to, and creates meaningful improvement in our schools. The goal is to transform the

> *Let's change this process into something that builds relationships, is looked forward to, and creates meaningful improvement in our schools. #MakingEvalMeaningful*

conversation to a process that outlines the next steps of professional growth for each of our valued faculty members. This change is difficult but not impossible.

This book will start by addressing a reality I hear very few educators ever address when discussing evaluation. Evaluation practices, positive and negative, have an absolute impact on the culture of a school. The second section of the book contains the core ideas around mindset, preparation, and skills necessary to be an outstanding instructional leader and evaluator. This will include the discussion of the necessity of a deep understanding of effective practice and the ability to not only identify and rate behaviors but to also be able to provide suggestions for improvement corresponding to critique. I cannot imagine an investment advisor telling someone that their portfolio looks proficient or that is does not quite meet standard and then ending the conversation and thinking that is sufficient. This type of behavior is common with evaluations, however. As professionals, we need to do better. The final section of the book centers on the feedback given to teachers. So in essence, the book flows from how to improve the culture of the entire school community, then to the work needed to improve individual evaluator performance, and finally to how to communicate to teachers so that the time and effort and energy put into the evaluation process can take hold and truly drive improvement.

As George Couros says in his book *The Innovator's Mindset: Empower Learning, Unleash Talent, and Lead a Culture of Creativity* (2015), change is an opportunity to do something amazing. And change is what is necessary when it comes to the systemic practice of teacher evaluation. If we truly engage in the process as instructional leaders, the opportunity exists to dramatically impact the performance of our teachers and change the product delivered to kids. Evaluation is our best chance to be instructional leaders, and this book will help take us to that place.

Realize Evaluation
Undoubtedly Impacts Culture

"[School] culture is the personality of the group, which is influenced by leadership, the community, the school's history, and the unwritten rules people abide by."

Steve Gruenert and Todd Whitaker

As a school leader, there must be the realization that everything we do serves to impact the culture of a school. The perplexing nature of school leadership, however, is that while every action a leader takes influences school culture, it is an entity that ultimately they do not control. This concept was impossibly complex for me to understand until I started raising my tween children. Everything I do has some impact on their attitudes, behaviors, and personality—yet, ultimately I have no true control in the person they will become. Being able to observe this interaction between extreme influence and lack of control with my own children helped me to realize the parallel with building cultures for principals. We influence our children, we do not control them, just as we influence our building cultures, but cannot control them.

CULTURAL IMPACT OF EVALUATION

If everything a leader does impacts culture (and I believe it does), then evaluation undoubtedly has a profound impact on the culture of a building. In my experience, evaluation tends to have one of three following impacts on school culture: lever or connecter, whip or aggravator, or a nondescript straw on the camel's back.

Lever or Connector

Great principals are able to use the evaluation process as a lever for improvement or as a tool for connecting initiatives. Almost all schools have similar initiatives taking place. Any of us could stand in front of our faculty and ask them to write down every initiative, directive, and mandate, and most schools would come up with a very similar list. *(*NOTE*—This activity is called an initiative purge and can be used to help explicitly form connections between all initiatives and align to overall goals. Activities or initiatives not contributing to achieving an overall goal can be considered for removal.)* The evaluation process too can be seen as another initiative, when in fact it should tie together every single activity taking place in the building. Simply stated, no activity taking place in the building should ***not be*** considered outstanding professional practice; this is precisely what the evaluation tool or framework should be measuring. Leveraging and connecting these entities is essential to provide vision and direction to all of the demanding work taking place in the building. As a specific example, if a building is working on creating and refining Understanding by Design (UbD) (Wiggins & McTighe, 1998) lesson plans, there are significant connections to both the Marzano and Danielson frameworks (Marzano, Frontier, & Livingston, 2011; Adams, Danielson, Moilanen, & Association for Supervision and Curriculum Development, 2009; Danielson, 2015) in the areas of planning and preparation. The ability to infuse and connect these two independent "initiatives" (UbD and evaluation) for a teacher can paint a picture that serves to drive importance and provide added direction. It is vital to remember that because a connection is readily apparent to you as an evaluator, it does not mean it is clear to the teacher. Making the connection is the responsibility of the leader.

Whip or Aggravator

In some buildings, the evaluation tool is seen as the whip or a weapon used against teachers. Many principals in buildings where this perception exists would agree that any time a teacher receives negative (*needs improvement* or *unsatisfactory*) ratings, this claim is made. This is profoundly false. The language, relationships, and commitment to teacher growth of the principal do far more to determine this culture than the assignment of a performance rating. Examine these two statements found in comments sent to teachers after informal observations:

> *A quality teacher always knows how each student has progressed toward attaining the stated goal of the lesson through formative assessment. Continued failure to master this concept will lead to subsequent needs improvement or unsatisfactory ratings for the teacher.*

Compared to

From the observation, it would be impossible for you to know if students really "got it." I think that a few simple alterations in your practice could help you to answer this question, and it could have a profound impact on the rest of your instructional practice as well. I am excited that we have this opportunity to work and grow together. Please stop by tomorrow at three, and we can work through this together.

In one instance, the observation or evaluation process is used to identify flaws and then to assert the consequences if those flaws are not fixed. In the second commentary, the same flaws were identified, but the evaluator stated these as an opportunity for growth. Moreover, not only were they referred to as growth opportunities, but the evaluator also provides support in a meeting and referenced mutual ownership of the teacher's growth. While receiving negative feedback is difficult for anyone, principals can go a long way to ensuring that, through their language and behavior, the evaluation tool is not viewed as a weapon but as a tool for growth.

One More Thing to Do

Unfortunately, the evaluation process is perceived as "one more thing to do" in most districts. Often, the evaluation process becomes the metaphorical straw that breaks the camel's back in terms of teacher stress. Evaluation is something that occurs whenever dictated by district rule or collective bargaining agreement and unless it is personally impacting a teacher, it is generally ignored. Under these circumstances, the evaluation process is a nonessential piece of school or teacher improvement—it is something all involved are simply compliant regarding.

This too is a reflection of leadership. If the attitude of the evaluator toward evaluation is about assessing someone's value to the organization as opposed to providing valuable information to help teacher growth—the process is mundane and simple. This attitude is nearly always reflected in writing and actions and determines the overall culture of the process. Leaders get back the behaviors they model and that they tolerate—modeling a dispassionate attitude toward the evaluation process will certainly lead to that culture within a building.

CHANGES

My hope thus far in this chapter was to convince you that, as an instructional leader, you and your actions make a difference. Most pointedly, I hope the takeaway has been that your actions in and around the evaluative process make a significant impact on the culture of the building. Making such an argument, however, does little to help impact the practice without tangible tips on how you can alter your behavior to achieve the intended outcomes of your building. Remember, when thinking about personal change, every system is perfectly designed to achieve the results it is producing (Nelson, Mohr, Batalden, & Plume, 1996; Berwick, 1996). Therefore, if you want to change the culture or success level of your building, the only input you have control over changing is your own behavior.

Thus, the acronym provided in this chapter (who does not want one more acronym to remember) is **CHANGES**. This acronym attempts to clearly identify **what an evaluator can intentionally do to have a positive impact upon on the culture of a building as it relates to evaluation**.

> **C—Coherent understanding**
> **H—Hook onto (connect)**
> **A—Always evaluating**
> **N—Not *to* but *for***
> **G—Give the work away**
> **E—Elevate everyone—see them for greater than they are**
> **S—Self-assess**

Coherent Understanding

Frameworks for evaluation provide a unique opportunity for evaluators and teachers to engage in a conversation about what great teaching is and is not. These conversations have undoubtedly taken place since the dawn of schools, but with an agreed-upon framework of practice the conversations can take on a new depth. One problem still exists, however. Just because two people read the same sentence, this does not mean they have the same understanding of what the words in the sentence mean.

The other night I told my son he could have a few friends over after soccer practice. In my head, a few friends meant three or maybe four boys. I arrived home to a mixed crowd of approximately twelve kids. I stormed into the basement and called him upstairs (no doubt embarrassing him). He came upstairs and looked shocked that anger was on my face. I snarled, "Who did I say could come over?" He retorted, "A few friends." At that moment I realized that not only did he listen to me but also that he did (what he believed was) exactly what he was supposed to do.

For those of you with tweens, teens, or older kids, this story may resonate, as you may have had a similar experience. The sensitive issue is that these same types of misunderstandings can take place during a performance evaluation that impacts someone's livelihood. One common example that comes up when working with the Danielson framework is what does the word *most* mean. *Most* is used multiple times in the framework and by definition *most* would mean 51 percent. In my head, *most* means about 75 percent—and that is how I evaluated teachers for years. Does that make me wrong? No, but it makes it unfair if teachers were not given a fair shot to know explicitly what their expectations were.

If I were recommending one leadership behavior to help shift the culture of evaluation in a district, it would be to make sure everyone is speaking the same language. Many principals assume that, since the evaluation process is high stakes, teachers will pay attention to the tool and use it for their own personal growth. Without leadership using the evaluation framework as leverage for teacher growth, this is often not the case. Great principals know that teaching the framework and working diligently to ensure that everyone in the building has the **same** coherent understanding of the tool is of the utmost importance.

There is a plethora of ways to accomplish the goal of having everyone "speak the same language" in regard to an evaluation tool. I have seen each of the below methods be effective, and I have seen each fail. The key to success—you may have guessed it—is committed leadership setting the tone that this is important and meaningful work. Strategies include the following:

- Choose one subsection of the framework and examine thoroughly at each faculty meeting
- A Google Doc and virtual meetings
- Consultant-led workshops to grind through an entire tool in a few days
- A joint teacher–administrator committee working together to create a document and share with other stakeholders

The point is that any strategy typically employed to help people gain understanding and come to consensus will work. This process, like everything else in schools, has more viability and meaning when this decoding process serves to connect research, best practices, and local initiatives to the evaluation framework explicitly.

Hook Onto (Connect)

Howard Gardner's research on leadership and frameworks for leadership success transcend any one domain or profession. His work, dating back decades, identifies the ability of great leaders to lead by telling a compelling story. His work references leaders revered in our culture, such as Franklin Roosevelt, and those often condemned, such as Adolf Hitler. According to Gardner (1995), and I tend to agree, effective leaders are able to truly speak to their audience (Gardner preferred the term audience to followers) through stories *and* then embody the traits discussed in their stories. Essentially, Gardner stated that leaders need to connect to both the heart and the head and then they must walk the walk—not just talk the talk.

The very best example of storytelling I have witnessed took place at an opening day faculty meeting in a district I was supporting. The principal—a mid-forties male, tall, with a deep voice and wide shoulders—stood before his faculty. He went through a few slides of his presentation before he embarked on an interactive activity. He posted pertinent educational data about students on a slide absent of name or identifying details and had teachers work in their surrounding groups to try and characterize the student the best that they could. The first student's data was that of a typical honor student on track to attend a prestigious university. Teachers collaborated and provided a glowing characterization. The next student—even better data. Teachers stated the student would have taken AP courses, was involved in the community, and had strong parent support. The next student seemed to struggle. He had a below 50th percentile ACT score and GPA. The student also had an uncharacteristic number of absences. The teachers buzzed and assumptions such as low-SES, ELL, and no parent involvement were tossed forward. The next slide—a picture of the student. The student was the principal's son.

In a five-minute activity—a story of sorts—the principal made the point that we cannot label and predetermine the trajectory of our students. He could have used any of the multitudes of research articles on teacher efficacy—but he did not. He used a story. A story I will never forget, and I am sure his teachers will not either.

So, how is this done in terms of evaluation? Leaders must communicate in a systematic pattern that Simon Sinek details in his TED Talk and which was referenced in the first chapter. All communication starts with the why, then details the how, and concludes by stating the what.

Consider the following statements:

The teacher needs to improve questioning techniques. Starting the lesson by asking higher-order questions would be a great start. This type of questioning should better engage students.

or

Student learning, outcomes, and behavior improve when students are intellectually engaged in the lesson. To engage students, our goal should be to force them into critical thinking as much as possible. Several techniques exist to help this to occur, but an easy strategy to employ immediately is to ask a handful of open-ended questions at the beginning of each lesson. To best increase student participation, make sure these questions do not have correct answers—this should encourage both participation and debate.

This simple example shows the power of following why, how, what—but it also explicitly shows the power of connection by linking improving questioning techniques to student behavior concerns, student achievement, and improved student data. Every comment is an opportunity to link everyday behaviors to overall mission, vision, and goals. Never miss a chance to connect work with its true meaning. People who are working with passion toward a meaningful goal are seldom those complaining of stress or fatigue. As leaders, we must work to supply the meaning and ignite the passion within our people.

Always Evaluating

One simple phrase should define our role as instructional leaders—"with awareness comes responsibility." Think about how many difficult or less-than-pleasant conversations we forgive ourselves of having on a daily basis. Each of those nonexistent conversations is a missed opportunity for growth. One of my favorite examples of the "self-forgiving" paradigm happened to me early in my career. One way or another, my school became embroiled in a cheating controversy in a prominent and notable competition. I spent weeks investigating, and it led to serious consequences for those involved—but throughout the evaluation it came up time and again that our alleged misdeeds were a result of our competitions. While this subsequent allegation had nothing to do with our predicament, it continued to burn in the back of my head as the incident concluded. I resolved that the best thing I could do was to call my counterpart in the aforementioned district and let him know that these rumors were swirling. I made the call, and the principal swiftly told me, "Well . . . it is Friday—and I am not going to get into that today."

While the above story seems hyperbolic, school leaders are confronted with situations where they have the opportunity to have growth-minded conversations every day. A few quick examples I often see:

- Students lined up at the door before the bell
- Teachers giving credit—or worse, extra credit—for items, like bringing in tissues
- Grading students based on parent participation in activities
- Coloring as an essential part of the curriculum

These examples are not to condemn typical teaching practice—but the above items are happening in a vast array of schools almost every day. In each circumstance, the principal must weigh promoting a culture of accountability, best practice, and attempting to live the mission or choosing the easier path. Let me assure you—the only person who wins when a choice is made to not address such situations is YOU. We often cite building political capital as a case against focusing on growth and evaluation of performance every day. We cannot afford to do this. Our kids and community deserve better. With awareness comes responsibility.

Not *To* but *For*

I was in my first year as a principal, and my evaluator was sitting in on a post-evaluation conference between one of my teachers and me. (As a sidenote, I strongly recommend this practice.) The evaluation conference went well in my opinion, or at least, it went the same as all others I had been a part of to this point in my career. In the debrief with the district office administrator, he told me that everything I said was technically correct—but I was trying to fix the teacher instead of help him grow. I was communicating *to* him, not *for* him.

I believe that he probably saw a light bulb turn on over my head. I simply had never thought of my role as an evaluator in that capacity before. That conversation forever changed the way I communicate and forever changed my perception of the role of the leader in an evaluation conference. This statement led me to have the most troublesome and liberating epiphany of my career. I did not control anyone's growth—I could only create the right conditions around each individual to support their personal journey. Like that, I was no longer in the business of "fixing" people.

The below table simply provides a few examples of moving from fixing language to supportive language. In doing so, a movement from communicating "to someone" to "for someone" naturally occurs.

Table 1.1 Moving From Fixing Language to Supporting Language

FIXING LANGUAGE (to)	SUPPORTING LANGUAGE (for)
Formatively assess students at some point every day.	Can I help you in figuring out what each kid knows at the end of each lesson?
Build better relationships with kids and your classroom management will improve.	How can we work together to make sure your kids know you care about them?
Status quo is not an option in this building. Continue to plan for your personal growth.	Have you ever seen yourself as a leader in the building, because I do . . .

Give the Work Away

Evaluation provides school leaders a systematic opportunity to help improve the professional practice of teachers. Teacher growth, however, does not simply mean growth within the classroom. Great leaders use the evaluation process to help guide teachers into advanced leadership roles within the school. Most schools rely heavily on the work of teachers to provide leadership and guidance to initiatives, programs, and continuous improvement activities. Leveraging the evaluation process to promote such work is a simple concept—but one that is beneficial in many ways.

Advancing leadership opportunities for staff through the evaluation process and in everyday action indicates the following:

- You want others to grow
- You believe in them as competent professionals
- You trust their leadership
- The collective vision for the future of the school is more important than your personal vision

Many leaders, however, struggle with the idea of advancing leadership by allowing teachers into the world of administration. To that, I offer this advice. First, ask yourself what do you do on a daily basis that is truly confidential and can only be done by you. Second, admit that you like control and work to move past that.

When I first became a building leader, I promised myself I would not delegate as if it was a good thing. I was always the person that was delegated to early in my career. I like to think that is because I got things done in a relatively efficient and effective manner—but I still despised the act of delegating. I would be hard at work in a building on a Saturday thinking of my boss sitting by his pool and grow angry and promise to never do this to my people. My issue, it turns out, had little to do with work and everything to do with perspective.

To explain, in my first year as a principal, a veteran principal stopped by to chat and check in on me. He asked about my hours and how my work-life balance had adjusted to the position. I told him my hours and he shrieked. He asked about several administrative tasks and who was doing them. The answer to each was simple—I was. I thought I saw where this was going, and I went on with my speech about delegation and how "I would not do that" to my people. My friend then asked two questions that forever changed how I look at this process. First, "Why did I deserve to be the only one getting better at my job?" Next he advised, with each task, email, or paper that came across my desk, to first ask, "Who could benefit most from the opportunity of completing this task?"

Wow—my paradigm shifted in a single moment. Great leaders did not delegate—they capacity built. I could do that. From that moment forward, I looked at each conversation, task, and problem to solve as an opportunity to route the work to a leader or future leader in the building. This mindset shift is most easily understood by this hypothetical and cliché example conversation often discussed in the business world:

CFO: What happens if we invest time, effort, energy, and resources into someone and they leave?

CEO: What happens if we don't do all of those things and they stay?

Allowing someone deeper into the inner-workings of an organization is a net win on many levels. One of the primary benefits of this will be the culture of the building. When many people feel responsible for the function of the building, many people will care about the ideals, beliefs, and norms governing the building. Great schools are deep in great leaders. And great leaders grow great leaders.

Elevate Everyone

As educators, I like to presume that we work to see the best in people. I say with confidence that we almost always do when it comes to our kids. I hear evidence of this very frequently when one would least expect it—when administrators are issuing discipline. Comments like the below are stated very regularly:

- You have so much potential. I can see it inside you; I only wish that you could see it.
- You are destined for great things; I cannot wait until you decide you want to be as great as you can be.

  or

- This is one mistake—this does not define you. How you rebound from this mistake will determine how successful you will be.

These same types of conversations, however, happen shockingly infrequently with the adults in our buildings. The evaluation process is the perfect opportunity to see people for what they can become instead of what they are, and to help make this a part of the culture of your school. Great leaders set exceptionally high floors for performance but never place ceilings on their people.

As an assistant principal, I worked for a principal who was perfect for me at the time. The principal took the role of big brother and helped to shepherd me through some of the seemingly obligatory growing pains associated with the job. As close as we became on a personal level, there were some pieces of strategy and school operations in which we had differing views. It took me until my second year in the position to have the courage to professionally challenge him.

Our administrative meetings were often loose, involved food and banter, and did not follow a specific agenda. I knew, however, that on this day a topic of concern would come up and predicted that we would have differing opinions. This topic was important enough that I thought this was the time to step forward and say something. The topic arose, I professionally disagreed, the principal supported my position, and the next topic was discussed. The whole incident took forty-five seconds and was without apparent stress. The rest of the meeting continued and eventually concluded, and the whole time I was giving myself mental high-fives for standing up for what I thought was best for kids and in doing so not impacting my relationship with the principal.

As the meeting concluded and people packed up their laptops and notebooks to head toward the door, I heard softly from my principal—now seated behind his desk— "PJ, stick around for a minute." My heart sank—in the ten seconds it took for everyone to clear out and for me to meet him at the desk, I thought about every possible thing that could go wrong. He said three words to me—"You are ready." I questioned, "Ready for what?" He explained to me that I was ready to run my own building.

In that moment, my entire five-year career plan went out of the window. At the time of that conversation, I had hoped to start looking for a principal position in three years. And then, I was suddenly given a boost of confidence by someone who saw me for greater than I currently was and—perhaps more importantly—greater than I saw myself. I had always believed that being an educator was the greatest job on the world, because educators have the ability to change the trajectory a child's life every day. What I learned that day is that we school leaders have the same opportunity to change someone's life with the adults we work with. What an incredible opportunity—but what an incredible responsibility!

Evaluations have the ability to condemn people for where they are or to help elevate them to where we want them to be. A certain cynicism hovers over the evaluation process—a cynicism that assumes every teacher knows exactly what to do to be incredible and that those who are not exhibiting outstanding practices are stubborn, lazy, or incompetent. Great leaders have the ability to avoid the pitfall of evaluation cynicism and work to elevate people in their own eyes, and thereby in the individual's personal lens as well. Every teacher matters, and every teacher deserves to be elevated in our eyes and in their own eyes.

The impact of elevating people through the evaluation process rather than tearing them down by simply assigning a rating and attempting to justify the rating through data is profound. This process allows teachers to know that everyone is on the same team much more than rhetoric proclaiming the same thing. Moreover, it simply makes a difference. Think about the possibility we have as school leaders to help change the momentum and trajectory of someone's entire career simply by looking at the adults in our buildings through the same lens through which we view our students.

Self-Assess

Throughout this chapter, actions for using evaluation to positively impact the culture of a building have been discussed. Before our behavior begins to change and impact school culture, it is important that we have a gauge of where we currently stand. Starting on the next page, several suggested self-assessment questions are listed with brief explanations as to why each question is important to ask.

Assessing Our School Culture Regarding Evaluations

1. **The mission and vision of our school plays a significant role in teacher and student discipline as well as teacher evaluation. True/False**

    Often in areas that are most important to us, we lose focus of what is most important to us. Mission and vision speak to our overarching purpose and goals—when our thoughts revolve around those areas, our behaviors are more precise and effective.

2. **I think about helping someone else improve his or her practice _____ times per week. If multiple, I spend _____ percent of my time thinking about helping someone else improve his or her practice.**

    This is just a good check to see if you are running your day or if your day is running you. Chances are if your day is running you, evaluation is a nuisance and another thing to do. Flipping this dynamic is the first step to any substantive change.

3. **I feel _____ when entering someone's classroom for observation. This feeling is the same whether or not the teacher is a high performer or in need of significant help. True/False**

    There is never a time where increased self-awareness is not a positive. When dealing with evaluation, it is important to be cognizant of your emotions and stress level when examining how you can personally grow into a better evaluator. As a sidenote, there is nothing wrong with being nervous—the key is figuring out why that nervousness exists and addressing the "dis-ease," not the symptom of nervousness.

4. **I feel _____ when someone prepares to observe me in a professional setting.**

    This question is simply designed to provide a dose of empathy. A great assessment to measure your natural level of empathy is available here: https://psychology-tools .com/empathy-quotient/. Even the most confident and competent teacher may become nervous or stressed during an observation—we should all work to never forget that feeling and to adjust our actions accordingly.

5. **My first emotional reaction to critique is _____. This reaction is the same/ different depending on who provides the critique. This reaction is the same/ different depending on whether or not I truly understand the critique being provided.**

    This again plays to the empathy card—but also helps evaluators remember that the reaction they receive from a teacher is not personal. Whether there is a general disconnect, an angry outburst, or BCD (Blame, Complain, Defend) behaviors, it has much to do with how that person processes information than anything to do with the evaluator.

6. **My emotions when giving critiques include _____.**

    Knowing how you feel will help you assess your performance and improve. If you are nervous or insecure, chances are your words are not direct and specific enough to cause change. If you are angry or aggressive, your message will often be completely missed due to the delivery. Understanding your emotions helps you to figure out how to best communicate for your teachers.

7. **The culture of my building regarding administrators in classrooms can best be described as _____. Is the feeling the same regardless of individual evaluator or does it change? Why? _____**

    This is a general attempt at a self-diagnosis. I encourage this general question be considered in conjunction with and compared to the other questions asked throughout the self-assessment.

8. **The percentage of my teachers in my building that truly embrace observation and evaluation feedback would be best estimated at _____ percent.**

    It is not about what you teach, it is about what they learn. This is something that evaluation frameworks have helped to clarify in terms of classroom work, but it is also a standard educational leaders must hold themselves to as well.

9. **Observation data is collected throughout the evaluation cycle, helps me to support my teachers' professional growth, and is viewed as vital for our school's improvement. True/False**

    This question is intended to discern if the observation process and classroom visits contain true meaning. Additionally, is a connection made between teacher performance and school-wide goals? This question helps to discern if connections are being made and whether or not a compelling story is being told.

10. **What percentage of proficient or excellent staff members have you personalized a PD plan for _____?**

    This question begs the question of why we are more concerned with improving the performance of teachers toward the bottom end of the bell curve compared to all teachers. Theoretically, moving a good teacher to great could have as much impact as moving a middling teacher to above average.

11. **I adhere to all district policies and procedures regarding evaluation _____ percent of the time.**

    This is straightforward but helps to call out elephants in the room for many schools and districts. Always remember, it is absolutely meaningless to have policies and protocols if they are not being followed universally.

12. **Is your system built to continue to produce excellent results even if you were to leave? Yes/No. If not, how can you make it so?**

    This questions speaks to sustainability and whether or not teachers are being developed into leaders in their own building. As Collins discusses in *Good to Great,* Level 5 leaders are the ones who are able to create systems that produce positive results even in their absence.

13. **In the past year, how many teachers do you feel anecdotally you have helped improve as a direct result of observation and evaluation? _____**

    This question drives toward the meaning of the process. If you do not feel as though you are making a difference through the process, it becomes very difficult to find value in the time and energy put forth.

(Continued)

(Continued)

14. **Teachers invite you in to watch them try new instructional techniques. True/False**

    This speaks directly to the culture of innovation and partnership within your building. First and foremost, something new or innovative must be taking place in order to get an invitation. Second, trust must exist for someone to invite you to into their classroom, particularly when trying something new.

15. **The evaluation process is seen as the most vital element of your school improvement plan. True/False. If false, could it be? Why or why not?**

    In the healthiest of cultures, teacher observation and evaluation are a key cog in the continuous improvement cycle. If, as a teacher, I have no way of receiving feedback on my practice, I simply have no way to improve. If teaching is not improving, learning is not increasing, and school-wide outcomes will stagnate at best.

You cannot control the culture of your building, but if you are not actively working to shape it, you are doing a disservice to any other leadership efforts you are embarking upon.

Tips for Tomorrow and Mindset Shifts

At the conclusion of each chapter will be a brief section with a handful of takeaways any reader can employ. One subsection will be labeled Tips for Tomorrow. These are tangible efforts that can be made to immediately improve practice. Of course, all of these efforts are discussed in more detail earlier in the chapter. The second section deals with more intangible concepts, such as paradigm and perspective shifts for the reader to consider. It is a wonderful debate to consider if new ways of behaving cause new ways of thinking or if new ways of thinking cause new behaviors. This section in each chapter will address both the mental and the behavioral queues for improvement.

Tips for Tomorrow

- Set a meeting with teacher leaders to discuss a plan to create a common language regarding your evaluation rubric.
- Take the self-assessment provided and share with other administrators and teacher leaders.
- Tell one staff member you have never before told where you see them in the future.
- Give one thing away this week that you normally do that someone else could gain.
- Write, in no more than ten sentences, a cogent paragraph synthesizing all major initiatives in your building.

Mindset Shifts

- Embrace the concept *With Awareness Comes Responsibility.*
- You do not control other people's growth—you can only establish the right conditions for people to grow.
- View everything taking place in your building as a funnel working toward achieving your overall goals.
- Challenge yourself to abandon the thought process associated with "fixing" other people.
- View delegation as capacity building and evaluate every piece of work in that light.

Visit pjcaposey.com for additional
resources to improve and transform schools.

Master the Technical Elements of the Tool

"The capacity to learn is a gift; the ability to learn is a skill; the willingness to learn is a choice."

Brian Herbert

When I first started working with administrators in my buildings and in other districts on the topic of evaluation, I was shocked at what (at that point) I then perceived as the lack of courage to engage in difficult conversations. I remember sharing this information with my bosses and to anyone that would listen. I thought I had diagnosed the problem with evaluation—administrators simply needed to gain the fortitude to have the really difficult conversations when they saw practice in the classroom that needed to be fixed.

I started working with Mr. Morris, a principal who was also a friend, on this issue. I advised that he attend workshops, read books on difficult conversations, and engage in "role-playing" conversations for seemingly hours. It would appear that we would take one step forward, then I would observe a conversation with a teacher and all of a sudden, we were two steps back. I began to think that maybe this principal just did not have "what it takes" to have these conversations.

I arrived early one morning for one of our work sessions, and quite frankly, I had a bad attitude. I was becoming discouraged, because there was a gap between what I was certain Mr. Morris knew how to do in terms of meaningful conversations and how he would perform on "game day." I had grown skeptical, wondering if I had the skills—or if anybody did—to help this principal traverse that gap.

As I sat in his office to begin our work together, his secretary popped her head in and said, "Mrs. Burt is ready to see you now." Mr. Morris invited her in and went through the typical protocol about my presence in the room, and Mrs. Burt, a teacher, agreed to allow me to stay in the room. For the next five minutes, I watched as Mr. Morris had an exceptionally direct, meaningful conversation with Mrs. Burt regarding expectations on turning in lesson plans and arriving promptly at the agreed-upon start time. I was shocked. This was the type of conversation we had been practicing for months, and here it was taking place in front of my eyes!

The conversation was wrapping up, and a huge light bulb must have illuminated above my head. I wondered if the same thing happened for Mr. Morris. Mrs. Burt left, and I asked if he too realized what he just did. He nodded with affirmation. This principal was able to be direct and provide meaningful guidance, because of the confidence he had in his argument. It is a pretty clear line—if an employee is to be at work by 7:35, at 7:36, they are late. Holding someone accountable and providing guidance was not difficult for Mr. Morris, at this point. This understanding helped me realize that we were combating the wrong issue throughout the entirety of my work.

The issue that Mr. Morris had was that he did not have the confidence to lead complex conversations when it came to curriculum and instruction. He had never viewed himself as an instructional expert, despite being an award-winning teacher, and while he could recognize both wonderful and less-than-satisfactory practice, that is really all he could do. He could not take the next step to having meaningful conversations with teachers about their practice and helping them grow. The wonderful part of this being the issue is that learning more about instructional practice and best practice strategies is an eminently learnable skill.

Gaining a mastery over the content in the frameworks provides confidence and a depth of knowledge necessary to move teachers forward. Many evaluators make an assumption about their level of understanding of curriculum, instruction, and the evaluation frameworks and often have a very fixed or rigid mindset about learning. Some principals believe based on their prior experience in the classroom or in a curriculum-related position that they have vast mastery over all elements of pedagogy and do not need to learn the ins and outs of the evaluation frameworks. Others feel that they were never instructional experts and thereby the act of learning the frameworks would be futile. Neither is accurate.

The evaluation frameworks most districts are using, namely Danielson, Marzano, or a hybrid, are complex documents that do a superb job of capturing what it means to be an outstanding teacher. Both frameworks, however, have nuances and complexities that even the most seasoned instructor could learn from. Additionally, diving into either framework with fervor allows for an evaluator to move toward more objective practices of assigning a rating. Likewise, for those who feel less confident, the frameworks do a brilliant job of deconstructing teacher practice into smaller fragments that allow someone who is willing and eager to learn more about instructional practices and thereby help teachers grow.

CLOSE READING

When the Common Core State Standards or Next Generation Science Standards or any other set of standards are released, teachers are often tasked with reading, interpreting, and analyzing the information to identify the most important elements of each standard. The common vernacular for this in educational circles is "unwrapping" or "unpacking" standards. Larry Ainsworth (2015) is a leader in this field of work (along with formative assessment) and says that teachers of all grade levels can use unwrapping to deconstruct the wording of any standard to understand the full meaning. Ainsworth continues to explain that, by identifying the area to teach (noun) and then the description of how to teach it (verbs), a standard becomes unwrapped and teacher knowledge grows and decision making is made easier.

So, what does unpacking or unwrapping standards have to do with teacher evaluation? The frameworks, however brilliantly constructed, still are not abundantly clear when read in isolation. Not only do they sometimes contain a vast amount of jargon, they often use words that can have multiple meanings or interpretations. Therefore, undertaking a similar practice of unwrapping not only can help to clarify the desired outcomes for teachers and evaluators alike, but the process also helps to identify the practices that are most important to look and listen for during classroom observations. Table 2.1 indicates what a template may look like to support this process, based on the questioning and discussion techniques from 3b of the Danielson framework (Danielsongroup.org, n.d.), with a **few** (non-exhaustive) examples provided in italics. This table, as a template for future use, will continue to be built upon as the chapter progresses.

Most of teacher's questions/prompts are of high quality and support the lesson objectives, with adequate time for students to respond. A variety or series of questions/prompts are used to challenge students cognitively and advance high-level thinking and discourse. Teacher creates a genuine discussion among students, stepping aside when appropriate. Teacher successfully engages all students in the discussion, employing a range of strategies to ensure that all students are heard.

Table 2.1 Sample Domain/Component

Teacher Behaviors	
What do teachers need to do to?	**To what extent do they need to do it?**
Use everyday language—not evaluation-ese	Use everyday language—not evaluation-ese
(Focus on verbs—both written and implicit)	(Focus on adjectives and adverbs)
Ask questions or give prompts supporting lesson objectives	*High quality (good) and most (over half)*
	Adequate (at least 3 seconds)
Allow wait time	
Student Behaviors	
What do students need to do?	**To what extent do they need to do it?**
Engage in a discussion with other students	*Genuine (a true conversation with give and take)*
Be challenged cognitively	*All students*
	Use upper level of Bloom's (high-level thinking)

TIME IN CLASSROOMS

As with any type of learning, the best way to gain mastery is by applying what you have learned in a real-life setting. Unfortunately, for most evaluators, the first time you are sitting in a classroom observing a teacher you are doing so in an official capacity. I liken this to allowing someone to drive without ever having a behind-the-wheel experience. Sure, there are things to be taught in the classroom for driver's education, but there is a reason all states mandate some time behind the wheel with someone experienced before taking to the road alone. Unfortunately, the same cannot be said for most states when it comes to teacher evaluations.

Even for those evaluators who are experienced—but upon self-reflection realize their mastery of the framework or understanding of instructional practices is not extremely strong—there is no better way to grow than spending time in classrooms. With time in classrooms comes the ability to witness outstanding practice. I believe in education, and I believe in schools and teachers. In every building in every small town and large city, there is truly exceptional practice taking place. There is simply no better way to learn about great instruction than to witness it and collaboratively discuss with peers and colleagues.

When spending time in classrooms, specifically for the purpose of learning and growing as an evaluator, the best possible use of time is attempting to link particular behaviors, strategies, and typical classroom occurrences to specific parts of the framework and then measure effectiveness. Neither part is easy, but what many people do is focus on simply trying to figure out where something fits into the framework or under which design question and move forward. For example, when growing familiar with the frameworks, a teacher will ask a question and immediately an evaluator will label it is as coming from 3b in Danielson or Design Question 9 or Standard 5 in Marzano. Additional time in the classroom will help the evaluator to identify "look-fors" and "listen-fors." These are indicators that evaluators can use to identify what observed data matches what area, but they can also help in understanding the extent to which something is occurring.

- *Tip: Many, many companies, organizations, and districts have created documents to this end. This is not something you need to create independently—instead, all evaluators must learn how to use this to become more skilled using the frameworks and providing meaningful feedback. As with any resource you consult—a simple online search will provide many options. The quality of the resources procured, however, vary greatly.*

UNDERSTANDING OF BEST PRACTICE

The term *best practice* gets thrown around frequently in educational circles but is often misunderstood. Best practice alludes to something that when done will procure the best possible results. Nearly 170 years ago, the concept emerged that doctors—particularly those working in labor and delivery—should wash their hands. Per historical reports, this assertion proclaimed by Dr. Ignaz Philipp Semmelweis was met with a vitriolic response, as it challenged the status quo. This practice, now common, is the norm in hospitals and doctors' offices. Many hospital rooms have signs saying "please feel free to ask your physician to wash his hands before treating you." This is because studies have shown through data that a doctor washing his hands before working with a patient yields better results for those whom he serves. Thus, if you are in the medical field, washing your hands is a best practice—and if you are not, it is still a pretty awesome idea.

CREATING A CROSSWALK

The majority of this book is designed to be "framework agnostic" and to readily apply to either the Danielson or Marzano evaluation tools. While the next two sections are still relatively applicable to each, the pure design of the Marzano tool is based on his research in effective practices, and it shines through in nearly all elements of the framework. Danielson, while rooted in research, is not as directly or pointedly tied to best practice, and therefore its users may find the next section to be of more help.

John Hattie and (prior to him) Robert Marzano have done the hard work for educators. They have crunched the numbers, evaluated the research, and helped to thoroughly explain what works when it comes to best educating our kids. Simply put, there are strategies that when employed help teachers to achieve the desired outcome of student learning. To paraphrase Hattie's research—the overwhelming majority of what takes place in schools is good for kids. The issue is that less than half of what takes place in schools is good enough. Hattie defines good enough as causing at least a year of growth in our students. This premise creates a different lens through which to view the educational world—it is no longer the goal to employ strategies that move kids forward. The goal is to employ strategies that move kids forward at a rate allowing them to be at the desired level of performance at the conclusion of a given interval of time.

While the work of Hattie and Marzano are often referenced and held in high regard in educational circles, the connection between evaluation and their research often is missed. Table 2.2 lists five strategies or influences from Hattie's latest research (2012) that are high yield strategies are crosswalked to match up with specific domain/components on the Danielson framework for teaching. As mentioned earlier in the book, great leaders have the ability to connect and leverage multiple concepts taking place in schools for their teachers. This is one small example of how this can be done. Additionally, when looking to communicate the why to teachers, simply reminding them that research indicates such practice yields the best possible student outcomes is (or should be) a fairly convincing argument.

Table 2.2 Hattie/Danielson Crosswalk

Strategy or Influence	Explanation	Relation to Danielson Framework
Teacher Estimate of Achievement	"My teacher thought I was smarter than I was, so I was." Attributed to a six-year-old If a teacher has high expectations and belief that all students can and will learn in their classroom, they often do.	Teacher expectations for student performance and learning can literally be tied to every component of Domains 1, 2, and 3 of the framework.
Formative Assessment	Using any of multiple strategies to measure student progress toward a stated goal and then using the data received to pivot and adjust so that instruction meets the needs of all learners	1F—Designing Student Assessment 3B—Questioning and Discussion 3D—Using Assessment in Instruction
Self-Reported Grade	Also called Assessment-Capable Students. Students who are able to assess their progress compared to a known benchmark or standard perform better.	3A—Communication and Understanding of Learning Goal 3D—Using Assessment in Instruction Also more indirect ties to 3B and 3C
Piagetian Problems	Knowing the ways in which learners think and how this thinking can be constrained by their stages of development. This knowledge may be most important in how teachers choose materials and tasks, concept of study, and levels of difficulty and challenge. Additionally, this speaks to the importance of developing successive and simultaneous thinking for students.	Multiple times in various domain/components teachers are expected to have students intellectually engaged. Any time this is called for relates to this strategy. Directly, this applies to three areas within Domain 1. Domain 1A—Demonstrate Knowledge of Content and Pedagogy Domain 1C—Setting Instructional Outcomes Domain 1E—Designing Coherent Instruction
Micro Teaching	Videotaping of lessons or lessons in a lab setting for self-reflection and candid feedback	4A—Reflecting on Teaching 4D—Participating in a Professional Learning Community 4E—Growing and Developing Professionally

SUGGESTION FOR IMPROVEMENT BANK

If you do not have anything nice to say, then do not say anything at all.

While this is not a maxim that should fit in the evaluative setting, it often does in an obscure manner. In working with evaluators, it has become clear that if the administrator does not feel they have anything valuable to add, they often say nothing. The issue being the practice they are observing is not always stellar. In my conversations with administrators, it is often exposed that they hesitate to provide any critical feedback because they simply do not know what to say. Their experience and the framework may tell them that the practice needs to improve, but without the skill set or knowledge to help them fix it, evaluators often opt to say nothing.

This section of the book is intended to demonstrate how an administrator, school, or district could create a bank of suggestions for improvement for each subsection of the evaluation framework. The best banks are the ones that are created collaboratively with teachers. Remember, the smartest person in the school is usually not one person. It is the collective whole and knowledge within the school. Work together on this endeavor. It also tends to work better when a positive spin is placed on the title, such as Examples of Excellence or Guide to Growth. A simple template like the table displayed below offers a great tool for collaboration and provides a depth of knowledge that can help evaluators engage, when before they may have ignored a potential area for growth.

Table 2.3 Sample Table

Domain/ Component	Strategy	Local Expert	Web Link for Resources

STAYING CURRENT WITH TRENDS

Best practice strategies to cause student learning are relatively stagnant. The dominant evaluations of our time are also stable, with few adjustments taking place every few years. This makes perfect sense. Great teaching is great teaching. The practice of helping people grow in their thinking and learning has not fundamentally shifted since the days of Aristotle and Socrates. So the question it begs is, why is it important for evaluators and teachers alike to stay current and up-to-date with educational trends?

It is simple—we are preparing kids for their tomorrow and need to do so with the tools and techniques applicable to their tomorrow. Additionally, new tools and techniques are designed specifically to make things easier for teachers, not harder. For many, there may be a learning curve, but once a base level of proficiency is reached with many technological tools, it supports growth in teacher practice.

Think of some fundamental shifts that have occurred that once were met with the same criticism that particular apps and social media mediums meet today:

- Email compared to written letters and memos
- Electronic grade books compared to figuring grades by hand
- Smart boards compared to overheads
- Instant access to video compared to film strips

There are a plethora of more examples to share, but the point has been made. Great evaluators not only see teachers for greater than they currently are, but they also help them to see the future in their practice. Looking to the future also helps to establish the culture of a building to not accept the status quo and to never be satisfied with current performance. There is and will always be something we can do that better serves our students and community—or better prepares them for their tomorrow, even if it does not directly impact student achievement.

Tips for Tomorrow and Mindset Shifts

Tips for Tomorrow

- Closely read and analyze the framework of choice for your school or district—DO NOT forgive yourself of this responsibility.
- One step at a time. Pick a small section of the tool and commit to getting a little better each day.
- Start developing a bank of suggestions for improvement—remember our goal is to add value to teachers, not simply provide critique.
- Work to clarify what vague language and jargon *really* means and share with your teachers.
- Set the template for creating a crosswalk between best practice, current initiatives, and your evaluation framework.

Mindset Shifts

- Embrace the concept—With Awareness Comes Responsibility
- Confidence in technical skill breeds the willingness to engage in difficult conversations.
- Teaching and learning the framework is everyone's job—building collective expertise grows the organization.
- There is no better way to grow in your skill as an evaluator than spending time in classrooms.
- Great leaders connect all things taking place in their building and explain why and how that links to organizational objectives or mission.

online resources

Visit pjcaposey.com for additional resources to improve and transform schools.

Leverage the Opportunity Presented at a Pre-conference

"Were all instructors to realize that the quality of mental process, not the production of correct answers, is the measure of educative growth something hardly less than a revolution in teaching would be worked."

John Dewey

It is always discouraging to me when I ask people to talk about the most important part of the evaluation experience, because almost never do I hear any positive feedback about the pre-conference experience. My experience of sitting in and observing the evaluation process has made it clear to me that the level of importance most districts and school leaders place on the pre-conference protocol is exceptionally low. Most pre-conferences are rushed, focused on the upcoming lesson to be observed, and contain only surface-level conversation. This is profound opportunity needlessly wasted.

TYPICAL PRE-CONFERENCE EXPERIENCE

The average pre-conference experience borders on insulting for teachers. These are strong words, but put yourself in this position. Teachers are notified of the evaluation scheduled and provided a list of eight to ten questions to complete electronically and submit back to the evaluator by some arbitrary completion date. Different teachers approach this process with a different level of fervor. Some spend hours carefully constructing thoughtful responses to questions, such as "What do you know about your kids?" Additionally, some teachers provide a copious amount of artifacts and data to prove they are accomplishing what any framework describes as proficient or better practice. For some teachers, pre-conference preparation may take upwards of ten hours and be a very stressful process.

Once the preparation is over, the pre-conference meeting is scheduled between evaluator and teacher. In the vast majority of meetings that I sit through, I observe the following as key characteristics:

- Little mention of the artifacts teachers provided
- Regurgitation of the same questions answered in writing prior to the meeting
- Discussion focused only on the lesson at hand
- Little to no discussion about past goals, objectives, or teacher growth
- A perceived goal of simply completing the necessary protocol instead of investing in the teacher

One of the key auxiliary benefits of the evaluation process should be creation of a building of true, collaborative relationships. The way we treat our teachers by focusing on "getting through" the pre-conference simply serves to waste time and opportunity. Moreover, it sets a horrible tone for the rest of the evaluation process. When teachers work harder than administrators during the evaluation process, it serves to destroy the credibility of the process and the evaluator. In order to shift this behavior, we must shift how we view the pre-conference process.

PRE-CONFERENCE VERSUS JOB INTERVIEW

One of the first things I was able to do as a newly hired principal was to make a hire in my building for a business teacher. I was so excited for this opportunity to begin to build my staff with the type of people I wanted. The only issue is that I had no idea what I was doing. I reached out to a trusted colleague and said, "Where do I start?" He replied like any great mentor would, with a question of his own. He simply asked me what did I want in a teacher. I replied with three items—I wanted someone who would continue to grow, loved kids, and could plan their own content, because the current curriculum left a great deal to be desired. My mentor said wonderful, now write questions that will get you those answers.

In essence, this was a beautifully simple concept as articulated succinctly by Dr. Stephen Covey years ago: Begin with the end in mind (Covey, 2004). I went to work attempting to write questions that would allow me to answer the question of which candidate best possessed the three priorities and characteristics I sought in a teacher. I struggled through this process, but over time have developed questions that have helped me in my quest to find the right employees at the right time. (There are many services, such as Humanex, that help schools and school districts do the same thing.)

The same effort and energy put into that process should be the same effort and energy put into asking great pre-conference questions. The lever for change is understanding why this is so necessary. If I asked a potential hire if they were student centered or content centered, almost every person is going to give me the "correct" answer. This is not to infer that they are lying to me, but it does not give me a glimpse into the deeper values and beliefs of the teacher. This is common sense, which is why on interviews, you often hear questions that give scenarios, ask candidates to think critically on their feet, and in most cases do not have a simple or correct answer. Transpose that process to what we normally see during the pre-conference, where the bulk of the conversation takes place around these central questions:

- What will I see when I am in your classroom?
- What do you know about your kids?
- Is there anything you think I should know about your students?
- Where does this lesson fit in the scope and sequence?
- What will the learning objectives be for the lesson?
- Do you have a preference where I sit?

The major issue with these questions is that they provide no depth for the evaluator into understanding the motivations and beliefs of the teacher. I often share this analogy with principals when trying to convince them of the value of the pre-conference. If everybody in the world that had a fever was given aspirin, told to rest and push liquids, the majority of people would end up fine. The bad news is that several others would eventually parish. We would condemn a doctor that simply told everyone with a fever to take an aspirin and stopped his or her inquiry at that point. As evaluators, however, that is exactly what we do. We often take the least complex solution to the readily apparent problem, prescribe that remedy, and move on to the next patient. For instance, a teacher may be treating the agenda for the day as the lesson objective. The simple response would be to instruct the teacher to write the objective in the form, *the students will be able to* . . . , as a result of this lesson. Then the evaluator moves on like the problem is solved. As leaders, we would never accept this as a satisfactory course of action or response in an interview, yet we do with our employed teachers working with our kids!

MEANINGFUL PRE-CONFERENCE QUESTIONS

The intent of this section is not to create an all-inclusive or exhaustive list of every pre-conference question that needs to be asked and answered during the process. The goal is to provide the reader with multiple questions that dig deeper than most pre-conference questions and explain why they are valuable to ask and what could be understood by listening deeply to a teacher's answer. This should allow for principals to move forward and begin to address true issues and levers for improvement compared to simple "symptom" answers.

Most questions in this chapter will involve a what, how, why question format. This allows for scripted, deeper questions to be asked on each topic.

What is Rigor? How does this understanding impact your planning? Why is this important?

Rigor, Bloom's higher-order thinking, and Depth of Knowledge are all synonyms for each other. While they do not mean the exact same thing, they generally refer to using a range of approaches to ensure students use critical thinking skills in their learning. As leaders, we assume that everyone knows what we know all of the time. Asking the aforementioned questions allows an evaluator to confirm knowledge, understand how they apply that knowledge, and then ascertain the teacher's beliefs in a particular area. Once all of that information is garnered, the evaluator can accurately provide the appropriate support for what the teacher may need to grow.

What will you be teaching? How did you decide that this was essential for kids to know and be able to do? Why did you select this instructional strategy to match this content?

Every teacher knows what they will be teaching when they are observed, but how many have made a strategic decision as to why this was essential for kids? As more schools are moving toward a skills-centric curriculum using content as a support, this question becomes even more important. The complex nature of matching outcome, content, and instructional strategy is vital to effective teaching. The conversation that stems from this question (in addition to previously acquired data and knowledge) should allow an evaluator to determine if the teacher has a de facto instructional strategy and/or allows the most readily available resource (textbook) to determine the curriculum. While neither of those decisions inherently means the teacher is exhibiting poor practice, they absolutely delineate the teachers are not using best practice. This is why the questioning is so important. In theory, a teacher could perfectly match outcome, content, and strategy together by complete accident. This questioning allows an evaluator to provide guidance that supports continued daily growth.

What is one thing you have learned about a particular student through data that surprised you? How did you choose to examine that data? Why do you typically choose to use data and in what ways?

When asked to discuss their kids, teachers often provide the rundown of boy/girl breakdown, number of students with IEPs, and some other common demographic features. The goal is for teachers to dig deeper with data, so that it impacts their planning and instruction to best serve students. Asking these questions ensures that teachers have internalized some of the data they have consulted. Inquiring about data that surprised the teacher means the teacher would have had to consult data that did not simply affirm their perceptions of a student. Remember—everyone loves data when it confirms their opinion. This question is intentional in trying to see if a teacher will embrace data that does not simply confirm their initial suspicions about a student.

The follow-up how and why questions allow the evaluator to gain a better perspective of the process a teacher uses to find information. I do not want evaluators to assume any proficiency but to enter conversations with positive presuppositions. Hopefully, the teacher has a well thought-out process about how they examine data to best inform their instruction. If they do not, however, the process of follow-up questions focusing on the *why* provides an opportunity for an evaluator to add value to the teacher through this conversation.

What are your learning outcomes for the unit of which I am observing this one lesson? How do you determine if the stated learning outcomes are "good or not"? Why is it important for learning outcomes to be presented at varying levels of cognitive demand?

Often, evaluators ask for the learning outcomes of a particular lesson. While important to measure whether or not those outcomes are met during an observation, a more sound technique is to look at the lesson from the respect that it is one segment of a larger unit. The unit objectives should show through daily and be readily apparent when performing the observation. To explain, if there is misalignment between the outcomes of the day and the outcomes of the unit, then a great conversation can take place. Focusing on one lesson alone prevents this type of conversation from taking place.

The secondary and tertiary questions attempt to get into the thought process behind the outcomes students will be attempting to reach throughout the lesson. Ideally, every decision is made strategically and with alignment to the overall goals and objectives of the course at hand. This will allow an administrator to delve into that conversation. This line of questioning also provides an avenue for teachers who feel hamstrung by a rigid curriculum guide or scope and sequence to express these opinions in a safe space. The design of these questions to spark open dialogue means that the evaluator must listen well and be receptive to feedback about how things are done in the building and/or district in relation to curriculum, instruction, and assessment.

What percentage of learning outcomes for the unit are reflected on the next assessment? How do you know if there is a fair distribution of questions per learning objective? Why, ultimately, do we assess students?

It is not safe to assume that teachers are skilled at curriculum and assessment writing. The teacher involvement at each level differs from district to district, but one area most teachers have a woeful amount of under-training in is assessment design. Thus, the idea—which may make sense to some—that if a content/concept is important it should be taught, feedback should be provided, and then it should be assessed, and on the contrary, if it is not important, it should not be taught, is not common sense. This question gets to that end. Is what we are saying is important for kids to know and be able to do at the end of each day a true reflection of the assessment? Essentially, if kids wrote down the daily objectives and measured their progress toward mastery of those objectives, would they have a comprehensive study guide for their assessment? The correct answer is *yes*.

The follow-up questions move from simple alignment questions to assessment design questions. A very well-intentioned teacher may have five equally desired outcomes for a unit he or she values equally. In my experience, the first time a teacher experiences an assessment analysis or audit, all five outcomes almost never have the same "weight" of total points. Said differently, it shows misalignment when 65 percent of all assessment points are wrapped up in questions for one of the five outcomes that the teacher views as no more valuable than the other four. Asking questions and examining artifacts takes time and energy—but these types of questions are the ones that improve teacher practice so they may better serve our students.

What is formative assessment in your own words? How does it impact your daily planning? Why do some people argue formative assessment is the most important element of instruction?

Research affirms the importance of formative assessment and the potential impact it can have upon our learners. Formative assessment takes place intuitively for many teachers and systematically for many others. Understanding how a teacher views this practice and what it actually is provides insight to help guide practice. In most pre-conferences, formative assessment is discussed, and sometimes the actual instrument (exit ticket, etc.) is provided to show that this practice will take place. This, in essence, is simply providing the right answer to the question. Deeper analysis is needed to see if formative assessment is truly making a difference for the teacher—and more importantly, for the kids.

Using any method of formative assessment is better than not, but only if the data is truly used. Any systematic approach to gather information that will lead the instructor to pivot their instruction and potentially move in a different direction is a wonderful formative assessment. This can happen in a myriad of ways, whether through technology, conversation, or other methodologies. Whenever a teacher stops, thinks about the information they are receiving, and changes course to better meet the needs of kids, everyone wins. Our job in the pre-conference is to ask deep enough questions to determine if this is truly happening.

As a point of note, a key element of formative assessment that at times is underappreciated (the questions above attempt to provoke some discussion) is the concept of time. Formative assessment and the willingness to use the data provided to pivot instruction means that time is flexible in instruction and learning is not. To explain, slowing down to reteach or accelerating because mastery has already occurred means the teacher is more committed to the students than the lesson plan. This is a massive point of stress for teachers, because it feels uncontrolled. Prepare for this type of conversation and be willing to ask probing questions to explore this in greater detail.

*What resources do you typically consult
when planning a unit? How do you intentionally
continue to expand your go-to resources? Why is it
important to continue to expand knowledge of those resources?*

This question is designed to give the evaluator a peak into the preparatory process of our teachers. We are fortunate to live in a time where the world is our resource. Teachers connect with teachers throughout the world via social media and access incredible resources when leveraging technology. Often, however, the only resources teachers use are within the four walls of the schoolhouse. This question is designed to provide insight for the evaluator on what the teacher is doing to find resources for themselves and for their kids. Essentially, are they doing everything possible to secure the resources necessary to best support student learning?

Great educators stay unfinished. Great leaders create systems in which their people continue to grow in their absence. Evaluators must see this as part of the process during evaluation. Great instructional and leadership coaches operate from the paradigm that the answer to every problem is inside each of us. The secondary questions should allow greater depth of conversation as to how teachers can work to best support their own search for better resources to ultimately support student learning. Success is when this occurs without direction and becomes a habit of mind and habit of performance for our teachers.

*What do you do to adapt assessments for individual
students? How is it possible to adapt assessments
and maintain the integrity of the assessment? Why is it
important to have a well thought-out philosophy on retakes?*

As schools move closer and closer to true personalized learning for students, the opportunities for teacher flexibility continue to grow and grow. The line of questioning provided above, again, provides insight into a tangible practice and also the philosophical and core beliefs behind the actual practice. There is often a great debate on whether as humans we behave ourselves into new ways of thinking or if we believe our way into new ways of thinking. These questions allow for an assessment of both so that you can provide necessary support on both fronts.

It is surprising but true that in 2017 there are still debates surrounding retakes on assessment for kids. I can pontificate about the arrogance educators exude when they feel learning is time bound and their responsibility is the lesson they want to teach instead of the skills they were charged with imparting upon kids, but I will not. Simply put, this simple conversation about retakes provides a great insight to many educational philosophies and will help a skilled evaluator better understand the entire belief and value set of an educator. Thus, while I just exposed my bias in this paragraph, it is important for an evaluator to stay as neutral as possible. Communication that begins with listening and understanding the totality of someone's perspective always makes leading in any direction much easier.

What do you do to differentiate? How do you
work to differentiate up and down every day?
Why is differentiation important for all students?

Differentiation is like formative assessment in that it is discussed in many pre-conferences as currently constituted. Often questions such as, do you differentiate and when? are asked. Again, the correct answer is typically given and opportunities for true growth conversations are lost. My personal belief is that being skilled at differentiation is the most difficult instructional practice to master for teachers. I have observed amazing practice, but this is far more the exception than the norm. This difficulty also extends to providing support for teachers via evaluators. I believe that this is why it is often not investigated in depth by principals to determine what true practice is with differentiation. In hopes to provide a tool in the toolbox, great differentiation often happens in classrooms with the following characteristics:

- Skill acquisition trumps content knowledge.
- All activities planned for all kids lead toward the same destination, but the activities are tailored to meet various learners where they are.
- Kids are in charge of a large portion of their own learning.
- Lessons are high in student choice and low in teacher talk time.
- The classroom is a safe environment for student risk-taking and self-direction.

Oftentimes, having an outline of positive characteristics associated with an instructional strategy can help evaluators better engage in the process of providing feedback in a particular area.

FRAMEWORK ALIGNMENT

The questions provided are framework agnostic as they examine quality practices. The information procured from the questions and conversation starters above would allow an evaluator to accurately and adequately address areas of professional practice dealing with planning and preparation. As with all elements of this book, the focus is to create meaningful conversations and confidence in having such conversations as an evaluator. The questions and their direct alignment is not the most important component of this chapter. The most important component is to realize that there is a better way to honor and value teachers and the teacher evaluation process through the pre-conference. Educators cannot be content in missing out on this opportunity for wonderful, potentially career-altering conversations.

WHEN A PRE-CONFERENCE GOES WRONG

The purpose in writing a book like this is to help provide evaluators a plan for executing all elements of the evaluation process to their peak efficiencies. This subsection is designed to help provide guidance when the best-devised plan does not work and the system goes awry. Typically, this occurs in one of three ways. First, there is the simple evaluator's oversight. This occurs when despite best intent and preparation a subsection of questions is simply missed or passed over, leaving the evaluator without the data necessary to provide an accurate assessment of performance or to provide constructive feedback as needed to the teacher. Next, is the pre-conference where none of the questions asked are actually answered. While the evaluator should ask follow-up questions and not allow this to occur, it still sometimes happens. Last, is the pre-conference in which the teacher provides "all the right answers." I refer to this as the "textbook pre-conference." This provides the evaluator with the dilemma of trying to determine if the behaviors and beliefs of the teacher match the answers provided.

If the teacher walks out of your door and you realize that you just experienced one of the three types of pre-conference described above—DO NOT PANIC. The best part about the pre-conference is that it is just one part of the evaluation process. It is very easy to fold questions into the reflective conference, which serves the purpose of providing data that were not procured during the initial conversation. For instance, if you decide additional information is needed to understand the role instructional rigor plays on the planning process, the following string of questions could be employed:

- During the segment of the lesson where students were presenting their ideas at the board, would you say the majority of the class was cognitively engaged?
- How do you know? What is the difference between engagement and compliance—could you tell for sure in this lesson?
- Do you intentionally plan to engage students in critical thought in each lesson?

- Is this planning reflected in unit outcomes and assessment questions?
- Can you show me in the artifacts provided where this lesson fits and talk me through different levels of cognitive thought on the assessment?

One of the greatest misconceptions about the reflective conference is that it must be solely about what was observed in a lesson. Instead, it is a conclusion to a process about teacher growth. Anything and everything that could impact that end should be discussed.

RE-RECRUITMENT

The Studer Group works primarily with healthcare organizations to help them achieve and sustain exceptional improvement in clinical outcomes and financial results. By installing an execution framework they call Evidence-Based Leadership[SM], they believe organizations will be able to align goals, actions, and processes and execute them quickly. This framework creates the foundation that enables transformation in this era of continuous change. The Studer Group introduced me to the concept of constantly re-recruiting medium and high performers to our district. This process creates a different mindset for all conversations and helps leaders to go back to a lens of providing service to their staff instead of simply expecting outcomes.

The pre-conference can also be leveraged in this regard. Every chance we have to re-recruit our top performers and to invest in them is an opportunity worth taking. I have yet to meet someone who does not want to feel appreciated, invested in, and supported. The traditional pre-conference that is typically rushed through is not only a missed opportunity for those teachers that definitively need support, but it is also a missed opportunity to discuss growth potential and future roles in the organization with your highest performers.

Tips for Tomorrow and Mindset Shifts

Tips for Tomorrow

- Commit to the following norms of action in a pre-conference:
  - Do not ask the same question already answered in writing.
  - Review the documents and artifacts collected and ask appropriate questions.
  - Schedule the meetings appropriately: If a great meeting takes an hour—schedule an hour.
- Adopt questions as presented in this chapter or adapt to meet the specific context and culture of your building.

- Actively re-recruit one of your highest performers tomorrow.
- Read through interview questions and determine what interview questions you can begin to incorporate in the pre-conference.

Mindset Shifts

- Pre-conferences are vitally important to the health of the organization.
- Why and how questions need to be asked more than what questions.
- Re-recruitment should happen every day.
- Great leaders treat root causes of issues, not simply the symptoms.

Visit pjcaposey.com for additional
resources to improve and transform schools.

Possess a Game Plan
for Every Observation

"That's been one of my mantras—focus and simplicity. Simple can be harder than complex: You have to work hard to get your thinking clean to make it simple. But it's worth it in the end because once you get there, you can move mountains."

Steve Jobs

Evaluation frameworks have done a tremendous amount to help create a common language for evaluation and to articulate what great teaching practice looks like. They have, however, not provided extreme clarity for evaluators when they work to observe teachers. The training I received simply told me to take down every piece of data I could when in the classroom and assign them to a specific evaluation area—in the classroom, if you had enough skill—or at a later time, on your own. This made an already time-intensive process even more tedious when attempting to code hundreds of pieces of data after a twenty-minute evaluation. When evaluators adhere to the "blank slate" process of conducting evaluations, it often does not allow an administrator to see the forest through the trees. In an effort to document everything, an observer could not really observe the lesson with a critical, discerning eye.

A training my staff and I received from Dr. Richard Voltz of the Illinois Association of School Administrators suggested something that seems so obvious now but eluded my consciousness until that meeting. Simply put, have a game plan for every observation. Just as evaluators may have predisposed biases, such as focusing on student discipline or teacher questioning strategies, we can intentionally create a target bias for each observation. Strategically pick an area or two of focus and intently watch, listen, and learn in those areas while collecting apparent auxiliary data to better support a more comprehensive approach.

THREE TYPICAL OBSERVATIONAL PRACTICES

I was never taught how to complete an observation. I received standard evaluation training by the state in order to complete that portion of my job duties, but I never truly received any guidance on what I was really supposed to do. I believe we have all been there in that awkward moment of our early administrative career observations and evaluations. You open the door, it creaks loudly. The students' eyes immediately look to you as they momentarily lose focus on the lesson being taught. You look down and make a small hand gesture to the students indicating they need to focus on their teacher. Sometimes the teacher even stops teaching to introduce you. The rhythm of the lesson is broken, and you are the cause and feel horrible. Now you sit down with either a notebook or laptop in hand, and it is time to observe a teacher in action—but now what?

When push comes to shove, observers typically resort to one of these practices. The first is to immerse themselves in the lesson and take notes as the spirit moves them. We will call this the narrative approach, because that is typically what is constructed at the end of this process. Second would be the checklist approach. Checklists have been used in the observation and evaluation process for decades. The last approach is simply to document absolutely everything that occurs while an observer is in the classroom. Using this approach, which we will label the diary approach, an evaluator should be writing and documenting what is occurring at all times. Each approach has is benefits and drawbacks and can be used effectively when implemented intentionally.

Narrative Approach

As an educator who loves being in the classroom where learning is happening, there is almost nothing more enjoyable than walking into a class and simply experiencing the lesson as if I were a student. When I complete observations in this manner, I usually end up with several notes about the lesson. My notes, however, generally come back to two areas: Did students know what they were supposed to learn and could they gauge their own progress? And what were the number and types of questions the teacher asked? These are wonderful things to denote when in an observation. The issue, however, is that, if I only collect this data, it paints an incomplete picture. My bias toward the importance of student understanding of objective and of teacher questioning clearly shows through. Without a clear game plan, in a typical lesson I am drawn to my personal instructional biases. We all are, and we all have different triggers and stimuli that we look for with greater intent than others.

Table 4.1 Pros and Cons of Narrative Approach Observations

Pros	Cons
Enjoyable process for evaluator	Allows for personal bias to become the focus
Truly able to experience the lesson	Significant gaps in important areas may exist
Feedback is generally linked to an area in which the observer feels confident to provide advice, recommendations, or suggestions	Lack of data collected makes it more difficult for deep teacher reflection

Checklist Approach

One of my favorite books is *The Checklist Manifesto: How to Get Things Right* by Atul Gawande. A quote from Gawande that resonates with me in regards to teacher evaluation is:

> Good checklists, on the other hand are precise. They are efficient, to the point, and easy to use even in the most difficult situations. They do not try to spell out everything—a checklist cannot fly a plane. Instead, they provide reminders of only the most critical and important steps—the ones that even the highly skilled professional using them could miss. Good checklists are, above all, practical (2010, p. 120).

In my experience, it is extremely difficult to create a checklist that captures the essence of what is teaching and learning. I have found many checklists that denote what is

Table 4.2 Pros and Cons of Checklist Approach

Pros	Cons
Clear, objective measure	Misses context of the situation
Efficient	Often focused on teacher output instead of student reaction
Sound base for conversational feedback with teachers	Efficiency is lost if everything describing great instruction is included

good teaching, but few have been able to capture whether the sound instructional practices are resulting in student learning. And after all, student learning is the entire point of providing instruction anyway. Is it possible to create such a checklist? Quite possibly, but it would not be efficient or precise. As we see with both the Danielson and Marzano frameworks for evaluation, it is very difficult to adequately describe what great teacher practice is in a concise manner.

Diary Approach

The most common approach to training administrators recently is to teach them to record everything that they observe when they walk into a room. The observers have also been instructed to use words of precision over more vague counterparts. For instance, document that nineteen of twenty-one students were following along the correct page instead of simply saying "most students." The intent is to collect as much "data" as possible and to provide that feedback to teachers so they can almost relive the lesson through the eyes of a third party absent of bias and simply taking down factual statements. Once the data is collected, it is to be coded to fit in the appropriate place in the given framework, and based on the preponderance of evidence, the observer can subsequently assign a rating to a teacher that is supported by data.

Table 4.3 Pros and Cons to the Diary Approach

Pros	Cons
Data based	The context can be missed
Forced objectivity	Time intensive
Aids teacher reflection	Can seem impersonal

THE HYBRID SOLUTION

All three observation styles described above have merit, but all have drawbacks. While no system will be entirely perfect, a hybrid of the three systems above creates a systematic approach to observation that provides teachers with feedback in a manner encouraging reflection and supportive of overall growth. This original form of this tool was developed in my district (Meridian CUSD223) after our administrators received training from evaluation expert Dr. Richard Voltz; I have since made slight modifications.

Pre-observation Work

- Budget time. Time is the most important resource in schools and in life. Your schedules should match your priorities, and you should have a set amount of time you desire to spend in each observation. Flexibility is necessary at times, but so is structure. Attempt to stay to your schedule.
- Determine one or two primary areas of focus. For Danielson, this would be a component or two. With Marzano, this would refer to an element or two. For a modified, hybrid, or a completely different tool, this would be the smallest description of practice to which a rating is assigned.
- Print out or open documents that describe the components, elements, and so forth that you picked to focus on. The critical attributes provided by Danielson work perfectly, as do the scales and evidence documents provided in the Marzano tool.

Elements of an Effective Classroom Observation

- The opening minutes of an observation are a perfect time to collect very intentional, checklist-type data and to best prepare yourself for the next stages of the observation. Data to be collected include the following:
  - Number of students in the class
  - Description of the seating arrangement
  - Technology being used
  - Description of the physical setting—display of student work, posted objectives or rules
  - Note if it is clear as an observer if the desired outcome of the lesson has been communicated
  - Remind yourself to sit with your eyes on the students
- The "body" of the observation should include multiple components to help capture data and the essence of the lesson:
  - Diary-type data should be collected for a period of time—with particular attention to the predetermined areas of focus (three minutes or so)
  - Narrative-type data should be collected for a period of time—with particular attention to the predetermined areas of focus (three minutes or so)
  - The observer should engage students during their time in the classroom, if appropriate, in the natural pace of the lesson. (This is a cultural shift in many places and should be proactively addressed with teachers.) Appropriate questions include but are not limited to the following:
    - Please explain to me the purpose of the activity or lesson.
    - What are you learning?
    - How will the teacher know if you got the lesson or not?

- How will you know if you got it or not, and if you got it to the teacher's standards?
- What will the teacher do if you do not get it?
- What does the teacher normally do if you already know it?
  - ➢ *The overlap with the guiding questions of the PLC is very intentional.*

- Observation Closure
  - ○ Prepare to provide your teacher with six items as you leave the room:
    - The answer to the question, Was the lesson a success? To answer affirmatively, you must know the objective of the lesson and be able to track students' progress toward attainment of that benchmark.
    - A highlighted version of the paperwork brought in (scales and evidence or critical attributes) to denote the teacher performance in each of the sub-areas
    - A comment of praise
    - An area (the one you find most critical) that you would like the teacher to focus their improvement efforts upon
    - An open-ended, big-idea, reflective question
    - The notes taken during your time in the classroom

This may seem like an awful lot to accomplish in ten to fifteen minutes in a classroom. While I cannot argue against that comment, I can assure you that with time and organization this becomes much easier and quicker. My suggestion is for an observer to work within their district to create a document capturing these key elements of an observation to guide practice. As always, local expertise is best, so feel free to include any additional or exclude any previously included item on this observation protocol.

REFLECTIVE CONFERENCE IMPACT

Many evaluators complete great work in a classroom during an observation. The most efficient evaluators often have an email sent to the teacher with their attached data and feedback by the time their shoes leave the classroom. It is absolutely wonderful that the evaluator is in the classroom and efficient work is to be commended; however, assuming that email is going to make a difference is a large leap of faith. I liken sending that email and assuming it to spur action and improvement to someone receiving a late notice for a bill in the mail. Some people will get the notice, will have not realized the issue, and will work to correct it immediately. Others will get the notice, will have not have realized the issue, and will decide to work on the issue when convenient for them. Others will get the notice, deeply understand the issue, and will throw the notice away. If we deeply care about the growth of the teacher, we have a responsibility to follow up on the written information provided to ensure it becomes feedback for teacher growth.

Post-conferences and reflective conferences will be discussed in great detail later in the book, but I want to strongly suggest one element of practice for those completing (particularly) informal observations. Place a clean copy of the evidence and scale or critical attributes and ask the teacher to fill out the information highlighting what best describes their performance during your time in the room. This allows for the conversation to start in a logical place. Additional benefits are a deeper understanding of the evaluation framework and thereby the desired practice. By allowing for a more targeted conversation, many evaluators are able to move into the reflective conference with more confidence.

Tips for Tomorrow and Mindset Shifts

Tips for Tomorrow

- Create template to guide observational practices.
- Set a goal for number of classrooms visited.
- Always sit facing the students.
- Articulate to teachers that you will be talking with students during observations.

Mindset Shifts

- Identify personal bias you carry into an observation.
- Observations without face-to-face feedback have little lasting impact—commit to face-to-face debriefing.
- Schedules are to reflect priorities, and observing teachers and providing feedback must be a major priority.

Visit pjcaposey.com for additional
resources to improve and transform schools.

Create a Process
for Self-Reflection

"I think it's very important to have a feedback loop, where you're constantly thinking about what you've done and how you could be doing it better. I think that's the single best piece of advice: constantly think about how you could be doing things better and questioning yourself."

Elon Musk

I think every educator would say that there is a desire to be a reflective practitioner who critically analyzes their own performance in order to engage in a personal, continuous improvement cycle. The problem, however, is that when you reflect on behavior without a process for doing so or a benchmark to measure yourself against—it becomes a futile effort. To explain this concept, I often use the analogy of golf, because it fits in multiple ways.

I categorize my friends who golf into one of four categories. The first is the accomplished golfer. These friends usually competed in the sport or simply over time became very good at the sport. For the sake of this example I will call them experts. The next groups of golfers typically picked up golf in their adult years, love the sport, spend a lot of time playing, have a swing coach, and truly are striving to improve. This subset will be called the weekend warriors. The next subset is the group that plays eight to ten times a year, has a handful of great shots when they play, demonstrates some talent, but overall struggles immensely and becomes easily frustrated with the sport. This group is called the outing golfer. The fourth group are the people that play when they have to through work or family gettogethers and are perfectly comfortable not being very good at the sport. They simply enjoy the time with friends and family and like to be outside. This group we will call the hackers.

Now imagine one golfer from each of the four subsets hits a drive and it travels fifty yards right of the target and directly into a water hazard. Which of the four golfers do you believe could tell you why the ball traveled so far off target? Certainly, the expert would be able to self-identify and perhaps the weekend warrior as well. Most likely the hacker and outing golfer have no idea why the ball behaved in the manner which it did. In this circumstance, all four golfers could tell you what happened, but not all could tell you why. In fact, probably only the expert could tell you with confidence.

If you added a checklist or framework of what an ideal golf swing should look like and had each golfer self-assess again, potentially more golfers would understand what happened as well as how and why it happened. If the checklist itself did not provide clarity, because the outing golfer and hacker could not clearly understand the checklist, new options would have to be exhausted. These would include training on the checklist and perhaps a video review of the swing.

WHOA—This would be a lot of work to self-analyze and assess why one outcome did not come out as planned.

This analogy is formed because in education it often appears as though there is a belief that everyone should innately know how to self-analyze their actions innately. This is simply not the case. If evaluators want to use teacher self-assessment as part of the evaluation process, it is important that they actively participate in the process and provide support for their teachers throughout. This chapter will provide some suggestions and identify some pitfalls to avoid when asking teachers to complete self-assessments as part of the teacher evaluation and growth process.

SELF-ASSESSMENT DOS AND DON'TS

> *"Even if you think you're doing well and have it all figured out, there is a voice you will always inevitably hear at some point which nags at you and says 'but wait . . . ' Don't ever dismiss it, listen to what it has to say."*
>
> Ashly Lorenzana (n.d.)

Simply requiring a self-assessment as part of the evaluation process is not something that is going to change teacher performance. Using the example above, I could assess my golf swing all day long and not improve, because I have no idea what I am looking for and I am not skilled enough to even realize what is actually taking place during my swing. My golf swing is not far off from some teachers' ability to provide instruction. This does not mean they are not well intentioned or do not want to be great—it means they currently do not have the tools to accomplish that goal. Always operate from the paradigm that, if a teacher knew how to be great, he or she would already be an elite performer. Those that are not performing at an incredible level are not trying less hard or care less about kids—they simply need help and support.

A table is provided on the next page to provide a more comprehensive list of behaviors that an evaluator should or should not exhibit, but a few conceptual issues will be addressed in the text. The first item that commonly occurs and should not be part of an administrator's professional practice is using the teacher's self-assessment as a baseline. To explain, once many administrators receive the self-assessment, they begin the evaluation process from that spot. While the spot a person begins from on an evaluation *should not* matter—it often does have influence. The initial rating of a teacher should take place independent of the teacher self-assessment. Once completed, the areas where differences occur should be the starting point for meaningful conversation.

Next, it is important to give teachers the opportunity to talk positively about themselves and identify areas for potential growth. The Gallup survey for workplace engagement starts with the premise, "I get to do what I do best at work each day" (2016). The rationale for asking this question is the belief that full potential is only reached when individual talent meets a precise need. One of the existing issues in schools is the assumption that what everyone does best is teach. There are many teachers who have incredible talents that their students and colleagues will never know about, because they have not been asked about them and encouraged to demonstrate them. Asking teachers to talk about what they are great at (in and out of the classroom) provides opportunities to leverage incredible talents that an evaluator may never have known about.

Lastly, the self-assessment tool *does not* have to mirror the performance evaluation tool. There are many reasons why this makes sense (and it is a perfectly acceptable practice), but there are many reasons why creating a separate tool is also great practice. My hope is that everyone realizes that they do not have to do what is the least work or most initially intuitive. Critically think about what you want to come from a self-assessment and create the one that best meets your needs. For example, if the below six questions were the self-assessment, do you think you would get better or worse data than by asking someone to mark on "X" on each line of your designated framework?

1. What is your greatest talent inside and outside of the classroom?

2. When do you feel most comfortable in the classroom?

3. When do you feel the most uncomfortable in the classroom?

4. Who or where do you go to for help or advice?

5. What is the area you believe you have grown the most professionally this year?

6. If you could only be excellent/distinguished, and so forth, in one area of the tool, what would it be and why?

Table 5.1 Dos and Don'ts for Teacher Self-Assessment

Dos	Don'ts
Explain purpose	Substitute for own observations or use as the baseline
Focus on behaviors and skills	Focus on the performance rating
Understand that self-assessment is stressful under any circumstance—even more so when associated with performance evaluation	Ask for comparative assessment of performance
Include areas for commendation	Ask for personal feedback on any other employee or on yourself as the evaluator
Include self-identified areas for future growth	Ignore during evaluation conferences
Allow for (and encourage) identification of organizational areas for growth	Ask "too many" untargeted questions
Provide training on how to best self-assess—don't assume this is a skill	Have the employee simply complete an evaluation of themselves on the same framework
Make sure it reflects your mission, vision, values, and priorities	Be stagnant and/or over-value longitudinal data with self-assessment

GUIDED PRACTICE

When embracing anything that is new, of any moderate level of complexity, a model of gradual release of responsibility is never a bad idea. To liken self-assessment to an instructional lesson, it would be like handing the kids a rubric to assess their writing and never explaining it or providing systematic feedback to the student based on their work but expecting the writing to improve. It just does not make sense. There are multiple ways to help someone through this process, but I sincerely believe that the best possible action an evaluator can take is to critically analyze a video of the teacher teaching their kids. This provides for a "live" commentary, which allows for a teacher and their partner in growth (in this case the evaluator) to truly perform a critical analysis. Football coaches break down every play from every game at multiple angles trying to find an edge to lead to better performance—the growth that could occurs from a commitment to breakdown one lesson every month could be incredible.

UNDERSTAND EVALUATOR FEAR OF SELF-ASSESSMENT

Many administrators fear allowing teachers to have the opportunity to self-assess. It is important to understand that an inherent risk does occur when you allow for self-analysis. The risk is increased when the teacher is asked to rate themselves on the same framework or evaluation tool that the evaluator will eventually use. The risk is simple. Once someone commits something to paper in a self-analysis and the evaluator disagrees, the conversation becomes more difficult than if they did not. Often times, this becomes a debate or argument, and this is the type of conversation that most administrators try to avoid during the evaluation process.

Overcoming this fear is simple but takes mental energy. The fact that someone committed something to writing and shared with you does not mean they did not believe what they communicated before they did so. Simply put, this only adds a window into their thinking instead of going in blind. Additionally, if data has been collected and is used to support an opinion, then the conversation can go much easier. Below are a few quick tips when engaging in a conversation regarding a disputed evaluation rating:

- Listen—you may be wrong.
- Data is your friend; the teacher deserves to understand why you believe what you do.
- Remember, the objective is not to "win" the argument, but to help lead the teacher to better professional practice.
- If the conversation goes incredibly wrong—the evaluator still makes the final call. In the worst-case scenario, you need them to understand, not necessarily to agree.

AUXILIARY BENEFITS

In addition to providing the evaluator insight into how a teacher views their own performance, there are other auxiliary benefits associated with having a teacher complete a self-assessment.

Metacognition

As discussed in an earlier chapter on best practice, learning is amplified when people actively think about how they are thinking. Self-assessment happens constantly in our daily lives, and oftentimes, we do not take the mental time or energy to process what our brain is telling us at the moment.

> *"So few people are really aware of their thoughts. Their minds run all over the place without their permission, and they go along for the ride unknowingly and without making a choice."*
>
> Thomas M. Sterner (n.d.)

The process of making people engage in active self-reflection about their performance and how and why they approach certain situations in a particular manner helps to create learning. This provides for an opportunity for someone to potentially change their perspective about their own teaching. To paraphrase pop-psychologist and incredible author Malcolm Gladwell—each time we change our minds, we should celebrate, because we just became a little bit smarter (2005).

Framework Mastery

As a word of caution, any time we make the assumption that any framework for evaluation proactively being studied is guiding action for a professional, we have a high probability of being wrong. I hear this complaint a lot from principals I work with regarding teachers being unfamiliar with the evaluation rubric. When I ask them to detail what their evaluation framework states is desired practice, the room often goes silent. This discussion is not meant to excuse the practice of any set of professionals—but instead, it is to offer the suggestion to operate from the paradigm that teachers as a collective whole are studying and becoming experts on evaluation frameworks.

As a result, the process of self-assessment has an auxiliary benefit of helping provide teachers the opportunity to become more personally familiar with the evaluation framework. The process of self-assessment gives the teacher the opportunity to read the tool and critically think about their performance and the behaviors outlined as best practice. This process will engage the teacher in self-reflective and critical thought about the complexities of teaching—which are universally beneficial practices.

Perspective Is Added

Great evaluators and instructional leaders are effective, because they operate from the paradigm that the answer to any issue is already within the teacher. They view their job to help the teacher find the solution. Reading a self-analysis helps the evaluator to remember they are not going through the evaluation process to fix any teachers. Instead, they are working through the paradigm-shift as a partner and support. This process helps change the focus and lens of the evaluator, and this perspective shift impacts each and every conversation.

EVALUATOR SELF-ASSESSMENT

Self-assessment is not something limited to teachers. While I am sure that many principals go through a rigorous self-assessment process as part of their own performance evaluation, that is not what this section intends to highlight. Instead, I encourage that each evaluator complete a self-assessment after each stage of the evaluation process to ensure they are best meeting the needs of their teachers.

Table 5.2 Evaluator Self-Assessment

Pre-conference		Evaluation Write-Up		Post-Conference	
Did the pre-conference help to build a better personal and professional relationship with the teacher?	Yes No	Are all NI or Us accompanied by multiple suggestions for improvement?	Yes No	Did the post-conference help to build a better personal and professional relationship with the teacher?	Yes No
Did the pre-conference help build understanding of the evaluation framework for the teacher?		Are more than three components labeled "proficient," accompanied by suggestions for improvement?		Did the post-conference help build understanding of the evaluation framework for the teacher?	
Did the teacher talk 80 percent of the time?		Are the suggestions provided more specific than simply restating the rubric?		Did you attempt to build consensus for ratings to be assigned?	
Did the pre-conference require some type of self-assessment from the teacher—formal or informal?		Do you explain why areas for growth are important and how they can achieve improvement?		Did the post-conference extend beyond a lesson recap?	
Was the pre-conference dominated by WHY and HOW questions instead of asking about WHAT would be observed during the lesson?		Do suggestions for improvement link teacher to building and district goals and initiatives?		Did the teacher leave with concrete guidance as to the next steps for their personal development?	
Did the pre-conference focus more on the teacher than the upcoming lesson?		Are the instructional strategies recommended grounded in research?		Did the data collected prompt deeper questions about teacher practice?	
Feedback is information people receive about how they are doing trying to achieve a goal.		Does write-up demonstrate you know their professional journey and understand them as a human being?		Did the teacher talk at least 50 percent of the time?	

(Continued)

Table 5.2 (Continued)

Pre-conference	Evaluation Write-Up	Post-Conference
For feedback to be effective, it must be • Goal referenced • Tangible and transparent • Actionable • User friendly • Timely • Ongoing • Consistent	Is the tone of the evaluation neutral to positive, regardless of relationship or teacher performance?	Were accountability measures put in place for the next steps outlined for the teacher's professional growth?
	Do you avoid simply using "go-to" feedback?	Did I see a common thread in this evaluation to other evaluations I've done this year that would demonstrate a need for particular professional development within my building and/or other buildings in our district?
	Are concrete goals for improvement provided that directly link to suggestions for improvement?	
	Do you articulate your responsibility and accountability in helping the teacher grow in the future?	
	Is feedback for a specific domain/component labeled as such for easy understanding?	

Tips for Tomorrow and Mindset Shifts

Tips for Tomorrow

- Implement a personal self-reflection regarding the evaluation process.
- Encourage videotaping of lessons and partnered critique.
- Revisit the purpose for self-assessments and ensure your process matches your goals.

Mindset Shifts

- Self-assessment is not something people innately know how to do well.
- Self-assessments do not HAVE TO mirror the evaluation tool.
- Fear of teachers completing self-assessments is natural but must be overcome.
- Self-assessment is for teachers only.

online resources

Visit pjcaposey.com for additional
resources to improve and transform schools.

Be Cognizant of the Questions
Driving Effective Evaluation

"Success is nothing more than a few simple disciplines, practiced every day."

Jim Rohn

An issue in the world of education is that everything seems so big. There are no simple answers, no silver bullets, no magic spells in our industry. As a result, we attempt to create comprehensive solutions to complex problems, and as a result, the products seem overwhelming. Even Charlotte Danielson's group has issued a "chunked" version of her framework in order to better guide conversation. For the sake of this book, when examining the why, how, and what of evaluation, it becomes less intimidating to break these processes into driving questions.

DRIVING QUESTIONS

The driving questions are designed to guide the practice of evaluators when self-assessing their own work. The goal is for all evaluators to become increasingly proficient at their task, so that they can become better at serving teachers and helping them self-actualize in their profession. The purpose of the driving questions is to provide quality self-checks rooted in research that will help practitioners improve. While not every possible area of practice for teacher evaluators is covered in these questions, they provide a great basis from which to engage in self-analysis and to also create a backwards design approach to successful evaluations.

ARE SUGGESTIONS FOR IMPROVEMENT PRESENT ACROSS ALL DOMAINS AND DO THEY EXIST FOR COMPONENTS RATED *PROFICIENT* AS WELL AS *NEEDS IMPROVEMENT* OR *UNSATISFACTORY*?

The importance in providing suggestions for improvement to teachers when practice is proficient is multifaceted. First, it provides a roadmap toward excellent or distinguished teaching. Second, it sets a clear expectation that the goal is for all teachers to strive for excellence in all components. Lastly, it demonstrates an investment in the teacher. Often, if a component is proficient, a box is checked and that is the entirety of the feedback a teacher receives. This practice prevents the "box-checking" evaluator from simply completing evaluations because they have to—and helps to transform all evaluators into better instructional leaders.

The role of a leader is to set and clearly communicate high expectations for performance, provide support to help people meet those expectations, and then either celebrate the achievement of the goals or hold people accountable for not performing. Often when it comes to evaluation, we do not set high goals for faculty, particularly when people are being benchmarked against rigorous frameworks. Principals almost set a ceiling for performance by explaining how difficult it is to earn an *excellent* rating. The role often shifts from that of motivator helping people to reach higher, to one of counselor, denoting how proficient performance is okay. As has been said in this book multiple times—for a school to be great, there must be great teachers within the school. Leaders must set high expectations and continue to provide motivation and support toward these ends.

Principals must realize that simply checking a box denoting *proficient practice* without feedback on how to improve implies that no improvement is needed or that you, as their building leader, do not value improvement from their current station to what is possible. Failure to provide such suggestions is generally not a matter of know-how; it is simply a matter of time and effort. Evaluation, like most things in life, has a tendency to produce what you put into it. If you want the evaluation process to be meaningful as a principal, then an investment in the process and person being evaluated must be abundantly clear.

> **Tip: Write evaluations as if you were creating a playbook for excellent practice.**

> If current performance is Point A and excellent practice is Point B, the evaluation document should be a guidebook between the two places. If you are not providing suggestions for improvement on a good number of areas labeled proficient, then you are indicating to teachers that proficient practice is good enough for you and good enough for the kids you serve.

ARE THE SUGGESTIONS PROVIDED RESEARCH BASED AND GRADE AND CONTENT APPROPRIATE FOR EACH TEACHER?

One thing that is certainly not lacking in the world of education is a copious amount of research conducted and published. I am in no way condemning this, but simply pointing out that there are any number of studies that clearly point to strategies that when implemented have proven to yield results. Two comprehensive meta-analyses come to mind in this regard—John Hattie's *Visible Learning for Teachers: Maximizing Impact on Learning* and Marzano, Pickering, and Pollack's *Research-Based Strategies for Improving Student Achievement*—that explain numerous strategies that have statistically significant impact on student learning.

Within each of the strategies identified, there are subareas and strategies that can be identified and communicated to teachers as recommendations for improvement. For example, Hattie denotes self-reported grades—a function of metacognition—as a strategy that has significant leverage and has the ability to significantly impact student achievement. To explain, evaluators often do a much better job of explaining what a teacher does wrong, providing little overall guidance on how they can improve this area of potential growth.

> **Tip: Create a bank of suggestions as a school or district.**
>
> Administrators pouring through research and handing out a list at an in-service could complete this work, or it can be done in a way that is fun and allows our teachers to discuss their craft. A wonderful bank of suggestions can be created, in a collaborative manner that infuses technology, by starting a shared document or blog with a theme of the week asking teachers to talk about what they already do in their classrooms. For instance, the prompt "What strategies, apps, and resources do you use to help kids think about how they think in your classroom?" could produce wonderful feedback, which could be turned into a bank of suggestions for future improvement for district teachers. What is even better is now you have a colleague to pair a teacher up with who is an "expert" in each area.

DOES FEEDBACK LINK DISTRICT INITIATIVES AND GOALS TO INDIVIDUAL TEACHER PERFORMANCE?

The word *leverage* is used a lot in this book. I have found that when I use that word around educators, there is generally a negative reaction, with people feeling the meaning of the word *leverage* is too close to that of *manipulate*. As school leaders, I cannot think of a more important strategy for moving buildings and districts forward. Great leaders have the ability to create momentum to help achieve goals utilizing multiple stimuli—hence leveraging opportunities to create coordinated improvement efforts. The opportunity to link initiatives or areas of focus to the evaluation process is often lost.

If the areas of focus for a school is transitioning to Understanding by Design (UbD) units and infusing technology across the curriculum, there are almost limitless ways you can reference these initiatives and tie suggestions for improvement in multiple areas of the framework to these initiatives. In essence, you can help to promote the importance and relevance of the building or district initiatives or goals to the evaluation process. You can help unite the vision of the school with the framework outlining best practice for your teachers. Always remind your teachers that best practice instruction is not another thing to do or something we will ever be done striving for or another initiative.

> **Tip: Suggestions for improvement do not take the place of directives.**
>
> If it is a building policy that everyone must turn in lesson plans—then the first time someone is seeing that information should not be in the form of the evaluation. Evaluations and suggestions for improvement should support the building expectations, not be the only manner in which they are communicated or the only accountability measure.

DOES THE ADMINISTRATOR EXPLAIN THE WHY AND HOW BEHIND SUGGESTIONS FOR IMPROVEMENT?

A common practice for many administrators is to provide suggestions for improvement that simply restate the language in the framework. Let's use an example outside of education to illustrate why this is not ideal practice. The proper technique to shoot a basketball is with balance, eyes on the target, elbow aligned with basket, and with an extended follow-through (coaches will know this as BEEF). If a coach is critiquing a shot and tells his player to follow-through better—the coach is simply stating the what. He has neglected the how and the why. No great improvements will occur in anyone's performance if they do not understand how and why they need to change their performance or behavior.

So when evaluators tell their teachers to ask more, higher-order questions because that is what the framework says, they are essentially telling someone to follow-through better. Great principals do not operate with the assumption that the teacher already knows the perfect way to teach and is simply choosing not to. They view their job as a teacher and coach to improve performance by explaining the why and how.

Common Suggestion for Improvement

The teacher needs to ask more open-ended questions.

Improved Suggestions for Improvement

To best engage students, questions should be posed that create thought and genuine dialogue. An example of this would be, "Did you think that it was difficult to like Othello in the play?" This question does not have a right or wrong answer and requires an understanding of the character and an evaluation of their likeability. A question such as this requires higher-order thinking skills (think Bloom's) and would inspire debate in a classroom. Moving forward, I would like you to script at least five such questions for each lesson and include them in your planning documents. I would also suggest starting each class with such a question to immediately engage students.

The two examples (that is, the Common Suggestion and Improved Suggestions) mean the same thing. The second example simply provides a roadmap for improved performance and shows an investment in the teacher and a true commitment to their professional growth.

Tip: Every suggestion for improvement should follow the why, how, what communication pattern.

Great suggestions for improvement explain why the change in practice is needed and then how to accomplish that change. The last thing communicated should be what—which is generally restating the wording of the framework to concretely identify the area for potential growth.

DO THEMES OR TENDENCIES EMERGE?

Every person has a lens through which they see the world. Each lens is different and has been shaped by any number of experiences (positive and negative) and is being constantly shaped by continued learning and personal evolution. As a result, I believe it nearly impossible to think that any training or professional development will create perfectly tuned, blank-slate evaluators. In my experience, this is what most evaluation training attempts to do. While this makes logical sense from the perspective of allowing the evaluation to tell its own story, it also (in theory) may eliminate an abundant gift the evaluator may possess in order to preserve the desired state of being a blank slate.

Great evaluators simply need to be aware of their predispositions and biases and work to use them as strengths, while avoiding becoming obsessively focused on one particular area. To explain, I work closely with an administrator who spent the majority of his career in an urban environment and is currently working in a small-town, rural school. The experiences this administrator gathered through years of evaluation and professional development has led this administrator to be masterful when it comes to observing, critiquing, and providing suggestions regarding classroom management and creating an environment of respect and rapport. Instead of asking this evaluator to forget this as a strength, it is important to promote this within his evaluative work. The caveat is, despite his strength and "eye" for this in the classroom, he must stay attuned to the happenings in the total classroom and track data and provide feedback and suggestions for growth in all areas of effective classroom practice.

Themes also tend to appear when examining the teacher ratings assigned in written evaluations. There are two major themes I have discovered after reading an unbelievable amount of teacher evaluations. The first is somewhat innocuous. Evaluators have a tendency to over-justify high (excellent/distinguished) ratings and under-explain moderate or low rankings. Second, narrative feedback tends to not always match the assigned rating. This almost universally leads to the teacher receiving a higher rating than the narrative feedback would indicate. There could be a myriad of causes for this—but none of them are truly acceptable. We would not accept a home repair man that told you exactly why some appliance was not working at peak efficiency but then concluding that everything was OK and nothing needs to change. The same should not be acceptable for teacher performance.

> **Tip: Evaluate with a keen understanding of your lens and areas of expertise.**
>
> Self-reflect and work to understand and diagnose your true lens and predispositions when it comes to teacher evaluation. Once identified, ensure that you evaluate (lead) from your strengths, but be cognizant of this predisposition and do not allow it to dominate your thoughts throughout the entirety of an observation or the evaluation process.

Is There Evidence of Framework Mastery for the Evaluator?

Mastery is difficult to define for many things, including of framework mastery for an evaluator. Working through this process, I think one way in which evaluators can test their level of ability in terms of mastery of the evaluation framework is in light of the four questions of professional learning communities (PLC). With slight adaptation, the questions to be asked to best understand a personal level of mastery would be the following:

1. Do I have a complete understanding of the evaluation framework?

2. Do I have a complete understanding of how to assess a teacher's performance against the criteria established in the framework?

3. Do I know how to provide support for professional growth when teachers do not meet all of the desired criteria established in the framework?

4. Do I know how to provide support for professional growth when teachers meet or exceed the desired criteria established in the framework?

Table 6.1 Four Questions of Professional Learning Communities

Four Questions of the PLC as Popularized by Rick DuFour and Solution Tree
1.   What do we want kids to know and be able to do?
2.   How will we know that they do?
3.   What will we do when they do not know it?
4.   What will we do when they do know it?

Often, an apparent lack of mastery appears in areas of planning and instruction. Evaluators often seem less confident, as manifested through fewer concrete strategies for improvement provided in these areas. This may be a lack of mastery in understanding the framework OR a lack of confidence in knowing how to explain the why of the tool or the how of being able to better execute the performance outlined in the tool. Thus, until an evaluator is able to feel confident in answering each of the four questions posed above, total mastery will not exist. While this may seem abundantly apparent to some, it still needs to be said: Without a thorough understanding of the evaluation framework and how to help guide teachers from Point A to Point B in any subsection of the

Tip: Create meaningful suggestions for improvement to accompany each subsection of the evaluation framework.

Creating a bank or template of responses or suggestions for improvement is not "cheating." As long as the feedback given is authentic and matches the teacher's Point A and desired Point B, it will be meaningful. Additionally, consistent feedback throughout the building leveraging school-wide areas of focus can have a synergistic impact.

framework, it is nearly impossible for an evaluator to impact meaningful growth in their teachers.

Is the Tone and Type of Language (Direct and Indirect) the Same Across All Evaluation Summaries?

This may seem like a no-brainer, but it certainly is not. I will ask this question—and it is not meant to be simple rhetoric—who reads every line of every evaluation that another person writes? In theory, the answer should be the direct supervisor of that person. I can tell you with confidence that is certainly not the case in the vast majority of schools or districts. This is one of the "dirty little secrets" that continues to fester and leave a process that claims jobs, takes principals over 10 percent of their time on the job, causes everyone stress, and is not viewed as a key lever to drive personal growth or school improvement. There are no checks and balances, and there is no feedback for improvement from an arbitrary source to support growth.

In my work with evaluation, I try to help serve this purpose. When reading a set of evaluations from a given evaluator written over the course of either one year or one evaluation cycle (two years in some states), tendencies certainly emerge. One area that often materializes is slight tonal differences on a small percentage of evaluations. The majority of evaluations tend to have the same tone and word patterns and selection and tend to be similar in length. A subset of evaluations are often more recognizable as a result of exhibiting a more negative tone. Simple shifts appear, such as labeling practice as "fine" as opposed to "sound or proficient" and classes as "'disorganized" as opposed to stating "there were opportunities for growth in terms of organization." These are two microscopic examples of how the use of imprecise language can permeate, and there is nothing inherently wrong with saying certain practices are fine. There are, however, concerns worthy of attention when such language is an anomaly.

> **Tip: Always have a second person (same person consistently) read and provide feedback on written evaluations before you provide them to the teacher.**

Great evaluators read and reread their work to ensure no personal feelings of frustration or personal conflict are reflected in the feedback they provide their teachers. Consistency in message enhances your credibility as an evaluator and helps to ensure your ability to assess teacher performance without negative personal bias.

Does the Evaluator Provide Context and an Understanding of the Personal and Professional Growth of the Teacher?

The process of evaluation is essentially a process about change. Change is abundantly hard for a variety of reasons, and it is an incredibly trying and rewarding experience to lead this process. To use the metaphorical emotional bank account Dr. Covey discusses in *The 7 Habits of Highly Effective People* (2004), evaluation is nearly all about making deposits through support and investment and making withdrawals providing direct feedback and critique. If the former does not exist, it becomes very difficult to enact the latter. Earlier in this book, the role of evaluation on school culture is discussed. This is because evaluation can either buoy school culture or it can deflate school culture. The difference relies on the relationships built by the evaluator and the intent of his or her commentary.

Evaluation feedback should be *for* the teacher. This means that the feedback needs to be delivered with the best of intentions and carefully crafted to meet the needs of the person to whom it is directed. The best motivational speech delivered in Latin means nothing to me. Likewise, brilliant feedback and suggestions for improvement provided by someone with whom the target audience has no relationship may fall on deaf ears. When teachers perceive the feedback is for the sake of evaluation or for the sake of the school or district (often perceived when feedback is driven at test scores), it has limited functional meaning.

Great feedback *for* teachers should follow the format outlined in Jim Valvano's famous ESPY speech (1993): it must identify where the teacher was, where they are, and where they are going. This picture and context helps to make feedback and suggestions for feedback real. While consistency in how we communicate with all teachers is vital, it does not mean that our feedback should be sterile and void of personal connection. Quite the opposite. We should be kind and consistent in how we communicate with everyone, but a great evaluation tells a story of someone's career arc. The most important segment is articulating a vision for a better tomorrow for the teacher. Great leaders set floors for performance but never ceilings. See your people for greater than they see themselves.

> **Tip: Every evaluation should tell a personal story of current and future growth.**
>
> Work to make sure the written evaluation demonstrates the past growth made and paints a picture of a brighter future. An evaluation should not only be an assessment of value to the organization—it should also motivate and inspire future growth.

Does the Evaluator Provide Concrete Goals for Future Performance Outlined With Accountability Measures?

When working with teachers and leaders, I often ask the question, "Would we do it this way if we were sitting around right now and inventing school?" I think the way we provide feedback on evaluations is one example (of many) of a process that would certainly not be the same. Think about this—many schools, districts, and states have gone to a model in which any teacher receiving less than a proficient or satisfactory ranking must begin working on a professional development plan. The intent of these plans are to provide concrete methodologies and accountability measures in order to ensure the teacher takes the requisite steps to improve performance. Essentially, the goal of these plans is to cause improvement or the teacher may lose their job. All of this makes perfect sense to me.

The question then becomes, what about teachers that are—to speak plainly—just OK, or even those who are good? Our process clearly indicates we do not value their growth as much as we do those who are currently performing at a sub-satisfactory level. In less than 1 percent of instances when I work with principals have they identified that professional growth plans are issued for proficient or better teachers. So essentially, OK is good enough for our kids. Again, I ask—would we "invent" it that way? Not only does this send a poor message to your more proficient employees, it also defies much research on organizational theory and transformation. In Urban Meyer's recent leadership book *Above the Line* (Meyer & Coffey, 2015), he notes that spending the majority of your time on your significant under-performers not only is a poor strategy but also shows a level of arrogance and hubris as a leader.

When areas are provided, they are simply written on the piece of paper, and teachers are left for up to two years before they are evaluated again. This, for many teachers, means that their individualized growth plan is either nonexistent or is written on a piece of paper to be discussed once and filed away. This process is not one that builds culture. This process is not one that systematically improves teacher performance. This process does not indicate that the evaluator cares about the growth of the teacher for the sake of their growth as a person and professional.

> **Tip: Provide suggestions for improvement on at least three subareas of an evaluation marked *proficient* or higher.**

Proficient practice is not the goal. Transformative, life-changing performance from every teacher for every kid is the goal. Communicate as such, and provide a guide for growth for every teacher—not just the ones who are struggling. Move everyone from their Point A to their Point B.

Does the Evaluator Communicate as if They Mutually Own the Future Growth of the Teacher?

Passive attempts at leading professional growth are pervasive in written teacher evaluations. Comments denoting such passive performance may look like the following examples:

- Let me know if you need help.
- Please complete your professional goals and turn it in when convenient.
- Seek out PD in your areas marked *Needs Improvement.*

Comments such as these simply let the teacher know that they need to grow and you recognize they need to grow, but you are just unwilling to spend your time ensuring that growth takes place. Think about the conversation we would have with a teacher if we received a call from a parent who stated their eleven-year-old went in after school and asked for help. The teacher commended their student for coming in and then told them they could find their answer by checking their notes and completing a few Internet searches. The teacher did not offer to check in to make sure the student ever "got it," but reminded them it would be on the test later in month.

While nothing the teacher did was fundamentally wrong or horrible for kids—it was by no stretch what was best for kids. This is an important shift in thinking evaluators must make—fine practice is not fine. This goes for our teachers but *more importantly,* for us. The above scenario happens very consistently during the evaluation process for teachers. Evaluators often provide opportunities for improvement but stop their work at that moment. Great evaluators not only provide an opportunity to learn and give teachers the option to grow, but they also work their tails off to ensure learning and growth take place. Administrators must work as hard to serve our teachers as we demand our teachers work to serve our kids.

> **Tip: Schedule multiple check-ins post-evaluation to monitor professional growth.**
>
> Ideally, a professional development plan would be written, and within the plan, there would exist many accountability measures and checks to measure progress. If such a plan still does not exist after reading this book, minimally, take the time to set up periodic face-to-face meetings to meet and discuss progress toward goals stated in the evaluation.

IS FEEDBACK PROVIDED IN A CONSISTENT AND EASY-TO-UNDERSTAND MANNER?

Many evaluations are simply difficult to read. Either the feedback is inconsistent, or the feedback provided is consistent but not in an easily discernable manner. Examples of this include all feedback for a given domain being provided together without separation. For highly trained eyes, it can be difficult to read through a paragraph and assign given feedback to a certain area or subarea of an evaluation framework. Imagine how hard this may be for a teacher who only looks at the framework once every other year.

Evaluators should focus on increasing precision and the ability to be direct when communicating to teachers in writing through the evaluation process. A simple way to move forward is to ensure evaluators use a uniform structure of commentary when providing feedback to teachers:

- The suggested pattern would look like the below:
  - State clearly the domain/component or area/subarea of the evaluation framework.
  - Provide relevant evidence as observed or collected.
  - Indicate where that evidence fits in the framework—referencing elements, critical attributes, and/or component descriptions.
  - Provide a suggestion for improvement, unless the component was rated as excellent/distinguished.

- An example includes the following:
  - Domain 2A. Teacher greeted students by name as they entered the class and during the lesson. Students attended to what the teacher was saying throughout the entirety of the class and treated each other with respect throughout the lesson. As a result, the teacher earned a *proficient* rating in this component, since talk between teacher and student and student to student was uniformly respectful and the connection between teacher and students was clearly evident. In order to move to an *excellent* rating in this component, the teacher would need to demonstrate knowledge and caring about students outside of student life, students would need to feel empowered and actively correct one another on conduct, and the teacher must actively work to maintain student dignity at all times. SUGGESTIONS FOR IMPROVEMENT INCLUDE, BUT ARE NOT LIMITED TO, creating a survey to learn more about student interests and outside-of-school hobbies, attend extracurricular events and discuss with students, re-establish norms and expectations (i.e., this is OUR classroom not YOURS). The teacher has a responsibility to ensure it is a safe learning environment for all kids. Examples of a survey such as this are available in the teacher resource Google Drive folder.

Tip: Use a system or protocol for providing feedback focusing on providing a service to the teacher you are communicating for.

Skilled evaluators always remember that they most likely have a greater expertise in the framework than the average teacher and need to communicate for the teacher and not as if they were writing the evaluation to themselves. The suggested protocol would be to state the area being evaluated, provide relevant evidence as observed or collected, indicate where that evidence fits in the framework—providing as much detail as possible—and then provide a suggestion for improvement, unless the component was rated as excellent/distinguished.

Tips for Tomorrow and Mindset Shifts

Tips for Tomorrow

- Commit to offering multiple suggestions for improvement for all areas marked less than proficient.
- Create a standard template for how to deliver a suggestion for improvement. Use rules of positive feedback explored above and in depth later in the book.
- Create a standard goal-setting formula to work through with teachers.

Mindset Shifts

- Proficient areas deserve suggestions for improvement as well.
- Tone and bias are within all of us—work to be tone neutral when delivering feedback.
- Evaluator performance is more important for teacher growth than evaluation rating.
- The evaluator has mutual ownership of teacher development. We are in this together.

Visit pjcaposey.com for additional
resources to improve and transform schools.

The Reflective Conference

"Your work is going to fill a large part of your life, and the only way to be truly satisfied is to do what you believe is great work. And the only way to do great work is to love what you do. If you haven't found it yet, keep looking. Don't settle. As with all matters of the heart, you'll know when you find it."

Steve Jobs

The reflective conference should be the most important part of the evaluation process. Oftentimes, this conference is so dominated by nervous energy by both participants, however, that the meaning and intent can be lost. Too often reflective conferences devolve into a meeting that can be characterized in one of the following ways:

- Emotional reflective conference
  - This conversation is dominated by extreme emotion (tears, yelling, etc.), and the focus on improvement of instruction is entirely lost. This is not something that an evaluator can always control, but they have strong influence over it. It is important to understand that, once the conference has moved to an emotional state, it is nearly impossible for the rational mind to take back over and to have productive conversation.

- Competitive reflective conference
  - This type of conference happens extremely often and usually involves the evaluator competing with nobody in particular. This is the post-conference that is essentially a trial attempting to convince the teacher being evaluated that the ratings provided were fair and just. This type of conversation is almost always focused on the rating and not focused on growth or improvement.

- Know-it-all reflective conference
  - This conference takes place when the evaluator is simply trying to "fix" the teacher. Oftentimes, these reference trainings previously provided and tell teachers what to do. In the worst cases, these conferences focus on what teachers can do to improve their rating instead of improving their teaching.

- Get-it-done reflective conference
  - These conferences are more concerned with time than with productivity. It is ironic that teachers are often asked to focus more on student learning than lesson pacing, but evaluators make the same mistake during the post-conference process.

This chapter is dedicated to providing tips and strategies to help move past the stress of the reflective conference and the common types of reflective conferences mentioned above to help move toward productive dialogue that can serve to transform teaching practices.

FIGHT CLIMBING THE LADDER OF INFERENCE

Before the reflective conference even begins, an evaluator must fight climbing *the Ladder of Inference*. The concept of the Ladder of Inference originated by organizational psychologist Chris Argyris and was later popularized by Peter Senge in *The Fifth Discipline: The Art and Practice of the Learning* (1990). I personally have found nothing that better captures the process between observation and reflective conference when things typically turn unproductive.

- Step 1: Real data and experience
  - This is the actual observations that take place within a classroom. I like to refer to this as the video of the lesson. This is what actually occurred without bias or filter.

- Step 2: Selected data and experience
  - Step two is where we move from the actual truth to constructing our truth. This is where, as a human being, we subject the observation to our own lens and prior experience. We assert our personal filter to what we saw, and we construct new meaning.

- Step 3: Affix meaning
  - This is where we start to place judgment on the activities as we observed them. Some of these judgments include deciding whether and why some activities are positive and some are negative and why some have a benefit to the school community and some are a detriment.

- Step 4: Make assumptions
  - o This is the stage where we start to diagnose the cause of the problem or give credit to what is going well, without all of the information. This usually takes the form of assuming why something is happening without a discussion. This happens both positively and negatively whenever the ladder is being climbed. However, during evaluations, positive assumptions are often made whenever anything goes well. This prevents administrators from asking questions to ensure the positive practice they are observing is intentional and repeatable.

- Step 5: Come to conclusions
  - o This is the stage where we move from assumptions to identifying something MUST be a certain way. This is where our simple observation turns into a position. This is what leads reflective conferences to take on a competitive feel.

- Step 6: Reinforce beliefs
  - o Believing in something is powerful. This step on the ladder takes all information provided, which is insufficient, and uses it to reach what seems to be a logical conclusion. This is most powerful when a preconceived notion was already held. People tend to more readily believe data that affirms their preconceived notions. This is when the Ladder of Inference is most powerful and most dangerous.

- Step 7: Take action
  - o Steps one through six in this scenario take place prior to a reflective conference occurring. Once those steps have taken place prior to the conversation beginning in earnest, the conference almost always devolves. Fighting climbing the Ladder of Inference is one of the greatest challenges for evaluators but is necessary in order to have meaningful and productive conversations that can influence teacher practice.

The Ladder of Inference is explained in theoretical terms above. Here is an example of how the Ladder of Inference could play itself forward in a reflective conference.

Mr. Trissler walks into Mr. Teipel's room to complete an observation. Upon walking in, Mr. Trissler finds that the lesson is running well and students seem cognitively engaged throughout the lesson. The most recent staff development session focused on students' knowing the learning objective for each lesson, and Mr. Trissler looked throughout the room and could not find the objective posted. His notes also showed that at no time did Mr. Teipel directly state the objective per his notes. (Step 1) Mr. Trissler left the observation and was largely focused on this part of the data, despite the fact students were learning throughout the lesson and overall it appeared to be a success. In fact, when Mr. Trissler asked a student why they were doing this activity, the students was able to reply with ease. (Step 2) Mr. Trissler was concerned that Mr. Teipel did not follow the training provided and (Step 3) believed that this could be an example of an arrogance he had previously perceived with Mr. Teipel. (Step 4) Mr. Trissler reviewed some past notes before the post-conferences and determined that Mr. Teipel, although a productive teacher, must not value professional development, (Step 5) and this disregard for professional improvement was not acceptable (Step 6). Mr. Trissler prepared for the reflective conference and was prepared to make sure that Mr. Teipel knew this type of disregard for professional development would not stand any longer.

In this situation, it turned out that Mr. Teipel provided each student a packet to guide effort throughout each unit at the very outset of each section of work. For each day of work, the students were provided the daily objective, how it would eventually be measured, and why it was important for them to learn that skill or content. Additionally, he would post the material on various social media sites to engage students and parents. During the post-conference, Mr. Trissler began the conversation correcting the perceived misbehavior and explaining why that practice led to lower performance evaluation ratings in multiple categories before ever asking a question. The conference became argumentative and tense and ended on a negative note. It was not until Mr. Teipel provided copious evidence in his rebuttal that Mr. Trissler realized that he had climbed the Ladder of Inference.

Talk Less Than the Teacher

I have intentionally chosen to call the conference after observation the reflective conference, despite the fact many call it the post-conference. The intent of the conference after observation is not simply to meet, but it is to cause teacher reflection. Change in teacher performance only comes when teachers either think their way into a new way of performing or perform their way into a new way of thinking. The reflective conference is the evaluator's opportunity to make this happen.

A simple self-assessment to judge the success of a post-conference is to subtly keep track of the time each of you spends talking. Much the same way that teacher talk time (TTT) should not exceed student talk and/or thinking time (STT) in a classroom, the same can be said for a post-conference. While it seems artificial and contrived to keep track of the actual timing in this scenario, sometimes the "clunky" nature of this is what keeps us on track when trying to make a fundamental shift.

If simple quantification of seconds and minutes of speaking time is too generic or cumbersome for an evaluator, another way to evaluate the amount of TTT compared STT is to track the number of questions asked versus the number of statements made. This seems easier, since you can make a T-chart and fill it in with simple tally marks, but it is more difficult than some may think. The difficulty arises from the statement cloaked as a question. Simply put, just because something ends in a question mark—as in this instance—it should not necessarily be counted as a question. An example would be, "You need to start posting your objective on the whiteboard at the front of the classroom for each course you teach, do you agree?" Another way to look at this is whether or not you are providing a suggestion for improvement. Suggestions for improved practice accompanied by a question at the end should still be counted as a statement, as they are not used to stimulate critical thinking or self-driven solutions by the teacher.

TO SERVE, NOT TO CONVINCE

The following phenomenon occurs both in written evaluations and in reflective conferences. Evaluators are often compelled to argue or demonstrate the validity of their position when assigning performance ratings for teachers. This is one of the drawbacks in the conversion to the rubric or framework-based evaluation tool. There will always be a subjective element in deciding where the preponderance of evidence delineates that a person should be rated. While it is important to be able to justify the decision-making process, the judgment call is not the purpose of the evaluation process. The purpose of the evaluation process is to improve teacher performance. This focus is lost in many, many instances.

Below are a few tips to help self-regulate this behavior:

- In writing, provide suggestions for improvement that identify current behavior versus desired behavior, instead of explaining why current behavior equated to a certain rating
- Ask more questions (this is becoming thematic) using the rating one level higher to form the stem of the question. For instance, if the teacher is rated *needs improvement* and the description of proficient practice states, "most questions were of high quality and caused critical thinking," ask questions such as the following:
  - What questions could have been changed to provoke more critical thought?
  - What do you think a good balance is between recall questions and those causing critical thought, and how can you plan to reach that ratio in the future?
  - When is the best time to ask recall questions? Is it typically the best type of question to ask? How can we work together to form a plan to ask the same amount of questions but less that are recall only?

This line of questioning clearly indicates that the questions asked in the lesson were lower order in nature and did not serve to enhance the lesson. Instead of browbeating the teacher with the data, help them to see a path forward instead of trying to convince them of their less than ideal behavior.

QUESTIONS WITHOUT ANSWERS

A suggestion I often provide teachers after observing their lessons is to script at least five questions they believe will intellectually engage students for each lesson and build the lesson plan around those key elements. Many times teachers react as if this is a bit beneath them and that scripting questions is something for novice teachers. Data from districts I have worked in generally show that questioning is among (if not the) lowest-rated subsections of teacher performance. Still, there seems to be a presupposition that as educators we are good at asking questions.

This supposition also extends to administrators and readily shows itself during the reflective conference. It is ironic that a script of questions is followed to a disturbing level for pre-conferences, but oftentimes the reflective conference seems to be entirely improvised and driven by a handful of notes. I encourage everyone to script questions that cannot be answered in the following ways:

- Yes or no
- I have or I did
- By any specific number
- Re-stating a subsection of the evaluation tool

I also recommend a handful of questions to be asked at every reflective conference to simply begin the conversation. These questions include the following:

- How did you measure success of the lesson I observed, and why did you choose that as your metric for success?
- What do you think went best in the lesson, and do you think your students would agree?
- If you had a do-over of only sixty seconds of the lesson, what would you change and why?
- At what point in the lesson do you think the most kids were really thinking hard (Bloom's, Depth of Knowledge, etc.)?
- What is one section of the lesson you wished went better, but you are not quite sure how to change?

Simply put, enter the reflective conference with a strategy. Remember, the goal is to help teachers think critically about their own practice and for you to provide support. Script questions that you think will help engage every teacher in this process. Invest in the process to better invest in each teacher.

THE ANSWER IS WITHIN THEM

Education is not the filling of a pail, but the lighting of a fire.

Many schools have a poster with this message—a variation of words originally attributed to Plutarch (Jowett, 1892)—or one similar hanging in their hallways that provides meaning to the fact that students are not simply empty vessels but wonderfully creative and brilliant beings that need to be supported as they reach their potential. This fundamental belief, which guides the behaviors of all of the great administrators I know, often is vacant in the teacher evaluation process. It can become easy to forget about the potential and genius inside each of our faculty and staff. Sometimes we forget that all our people may need is a nudge in the right direction, some support to take a risk, affirmation of a vision, or just simply to get the heck out of their way.

The reflective conference gives us this opportunity. It gives us a formalized, systematic way to provide a nudge, help someone look inward, or to allow someone to share their dreams and ambitions with us. This conference is not about fixing our teachers. Our teachers are fundamentally not broken. If they are, then issues should be addressed long before, during, and after the evaluation process. Even the best-intentioned evaluators sometimes slip into "fixing" mode. Fixing language often leads the evaluator to reference themselves instead of something objective, such as "If I were you," or "You need to." Great administrators self-police themselves and avoid this language in hopes to evoke the solutions from within the teacher. There are times, however, when sound, best practices suggestions for improvement must be provided. The goal, however, is to do everything within your power to help the teacher find those suggestions with your support instead of simply giving the "answer" to them.

If the above scenario is difficult to understand, think of it from the teacher/student relationship perspective. Can you imagine a teacher sitting down with a student for a writing conference and telling the student to do these three things: write in complete sentences, use appropriate punctuation, and do not overuse the same adjectives. All of these suggestions have merit but in and of themselves do not fundamentally change the student as a writer, since the conversation has led to no greater understanding than before the meeting. The student may employ those strategies (assuming they even know how) for a little while, but without understanding why or having spent time thinking about it on their own, their long-term potential growth is limited, since the teacher simply tried to fix the student. This is the same scenario to be avoided as an evaluator.

SCHEDULES MATCH PRIORITIES

A major issue for both pre-observation and reflective conference meetings is that they often seem rushed. In order to not burden themselves or their staff with additional and copious meetings, principals often schedule these conferences for planning periods. With the assumption that an average preparatory period is forty-five minutes and that a teacher must close out and prep for a class, the conference would last approximately thirty-five minutes. In almost no instance is thirty-five minutes enough time to have a deep, meaningful conversation that digs beyond what happened or what will happen and serve to truly inform both the evaluator and teacher. This leads to a legitimate conundrum.

Time is the most precious resource we have in life and in our profession. The dilemma I challenge administrators to think about surrounds time versus meaning. If the most critical element of instructional leadership and school improvement can be done "fine" if you put in five hours per teacher, but exceptionally well if you put in six-and-a-half hours per teacher, what would you do? Assuming most principals do not formally evaluate more than twenty teachers per year, I just added thirty hours to your work life. That thirty hours can be added on top of what you already do, or you could re-prioritize your current schedule and ensure that your behaviors match your calendar and your calendar matches your priorities. This is a question only you can answer, and it is simple—if I had more time face-to-face with my teachers to discuss their instructional practices, philosophy, and professionalism, could I have a more profound impact on the overall health of my school? If the answer is yes—then change your practices to ensure pre- and post-conferences are not opportunities lost because of time constraints.

ESTABLISH GOAL AREAS

An entire chapter of this book will be dedicated to helping teachers establish goal areas for future development. This practice can begin during the reflective conference, or it can begin and the goals can be written and confirmed at the reflective conference. Either way, the reflective conference matters and should begin the process. This is a simple mindset shift for evaluators. Is the reflective conference an autopsy or a checkup? I think everyone would like to think the reflective conference will lead to future growth, so our behaviors must match this. Having a conversation about what has happened, without clearly defining what will happen in the future, means that, as the evaluator leading the meeting, we are considering the conference an autopsy of performance.

This process is simple and can be overt or subtle. It must be collaborative but driven by the teacher, and it must focus on improvement that will ultimately impact the students and the school. For instance, getting a higher rating is not acceptable as a goal moving forward. It must be a strategy that will help guide performance, which can be supported, practiced, and (hopefully) measured. While there are complexities to this, which will be examined later in the book, remember that the worst possible goal is the one that is never set. Support your teachers in their movement forward—nobody has ever been hired to maintain the status quo.

TIPS FOR SUCCESS FOR ALL
TYPES OF REFLECTIVE CONFERENCES

Reflective conferences can come in all shapes and sizes. Some feel like a walk in the park, and others feel like you just went twelve rounds with the heavyweight champion of the world. I try to encourage the principals I work with that it truly does not matter how you feel about it. What matters is how the teacher felt about it. When in doubt, always remember that Maslow's comes before Bloom's or any other learning framework or process of change. People must feel safe and supported in order to grow.

Argumentative

Argumentative reflective conferences can always be avoided. The desire of the person being evaluated to argue cannot always be avoided. As leaders, we influence situations; we do not control them. If someone is dead set on making an evaluation conference a miserable experience, all we can do it is try to mitigate the damage. Argumentative reflective conferences generally follow a BCD format. I first read about BCD behavior in Urban Meyer's leadership book, *Above the Line* (Meyer & Coffey, 2015, p. 29). When people refuse to take ownership or take the opportunity to leverage areas of potential growth, they often fall into the following pattern of rhetoric and speech: blame, complain, defend. A typical BCD reflective conference may look like the below:

BLAME: I have not started using (insert new resource provided), because our technology is so spotty in this building.

COMPLAIN: Even if the technology were better, it would be so hard to implement with all of the other new initiatives going on.

DEFEND: I have been doing it this way with my kids for years, and it has turned out ok.

Please note—this is not a behavior that is reserved for teachers or to educators. If you are a parent, does the next example sound familiar?

BLAME: I swear that (insert brother's name here) was going downstairs after I left, so I did not shut off the lights.

COMPLAIN: You are always yelling at us for the lights, it is not even that big of deal, and considering every other rule you have for us, it is hard to keep track.

DEFEND: It is scary to go downstairs alone if there are no lights on—you remember when we saw the mouse down there three years ago, don't you?

While BCD behavior is never productive, it does exist. If this is the pattern your conversation is starting to follow, there a few things you can do to ensure the best positive outcomes. First, if you have discussed BCD behaviors in your building and how they are not productive to outcomes or culture, you can address it directly. If you have not, this is probably not the time to employ that conversation, but it should be a mental note you make for a future conversation. Here are five quick tips to help you when a reflective conference heads down this path:

- Be empathetic (or at least compassionate). Remember the stress of the process and be quicker to forgive than anger.
- Do not take the bait. An argument does not help a teacher improve, and improvement is the point of the process.
- Redefine winning. Many leaders are naturally competitive, and winning a conversation is something that we often do not begin with the intention of doing—we somehow arrive there. Make a note above your desk, draw it on your hand—do something to remind yourself the only way to WIN a reflective conference conversation is to lead a teacher toward professional growth.
- Time: it is on your side. Moving a committed, educated person from a position that they believe and have been acting on for some time in one meeting may be entirely impossible. Many times principals work to impart fifteen opinions in thirty minutes. Great principals invest in their teachers, and the reflective conference (albeit extremely important) is just one component in a much larger process.
- Understand, not agree. If you are in an argumentative conversation, the goal should be to ensure the other party understands what you are trying to communicate, not necessarily agree. To be clear, this is not the ideal. But it is an option. And in this case, these are words worth uttering. "Ms. Burt, I am not trying to argue with you and I am not trying to convince you to agree with me. I do believe it is important that you understand my perspective on this." (Then, state your issue.)

Self-Analyzed

As an evaluator, we truly want teacher reflection. When I think of the ideal reflective conference, the teacher has critically thought through each element of a lesson and is able to accurately identify both strengths and weaknesses. The truly, deeply self-reflective teacher provides a different challenge for an evaluator, however. Here are a few ways in which a reflective conference can go awry with a truly thoughtful and insightful practitioner:

- Wrong reflection. Perhaps the scariest of the reflective practitioners is the one who seemingly lived through a different lesson than you did. This provides an evaluator with a unique challenge. When this begins, it is imperative to presume positive intentions. This means that we should not think that there is something contrived about this; we must operate as though their lens just saw the lesson in a different light. In these circumstances, data is extremely important. For instance, a teacher who thinks engagement was great but had only four of twenty-seven kids participating actively in the lesson.

- Reflection as a defense mechanism. Occasionally people will create an extensive reflection as a means of self-protection. I always think of this as the family rule. We can insult our family, but nobody else can insult our family. This manifests when teachers fear the feedback they may receive from their evaluator, so they feign a very reflective nature in order to protect themselves from what they fear may be criticism. The key to ensuring the conference is successful is agreeing to action and solutions, just not recounting what occurred. After all, we do not care how we get to a useful solution to improve instruction—but we just need to get there.

- Reflection without action. Reflection without action or intent to improve is a very tricky discussion to have. Additionally, this conference is almost impossible to have without personal experience with the teacher. Reflection without action often occurs after reflection as a defense mechanism takes place, without an agreement of action or when accountability is not present. If this is the case, the same strategy for a commitment to action from the teacher and accountability for the evaluator is prudent. Remember, always, that as the evaluator you are driving the conference. If someone is misguided or attempts to choose "low-hanging fruit" to work toward, it is your moral imperative to shift their focus to the actions that will most benefit the kids you both mutually serve.

Lost

I advocate that only teachers who are insubordinate or incompetent be "career coached" out of the profession. Insubordination is self-explanatory, but incompetent often is not. I believe in my heart that teachers deserve the opportunity to be supported and to grow. The reflective conference is a place where this can begin. If the teacher is totally lost—demonstrating a lack of knowledge about sound instructional and planning practices and with no depth of knowledge about the framework—it is the duty of the evaluator to turn into a teacher. Teachers deserve this and so do our kids. The other options are moving on from someone who may be exceptionally talented and loves kids or turning the other cheek. Either price is too much to pay. If, during a reflective conference, the teacher appears totally lost—remember that as an educator sometimes we must teach.

Nondescript

Sometimes, we are part of meetings, conversations, and conferences that are simply nondescript. They simply take place and then they are over and that is it. Often times, principals who I work with (particularly in challenging buildings) see these reflective conferences as a win. Survived it and lived to "lead" another day. These, perhaps, are the most dangerous of all. These are dangerous because this is typically what takes place when evaluators work with well-intentioned, mediocre to good teachers. This is an opportunity to help teachers systematically grow, and principals often forgive themselves of this chance in the name of ease, lack of stress, and a fictional gain in political capital. While everyone can think of a reflective conference that was contentious or one where it seemed the teacher was in a completely different room than you were, nobody remembers the nondescript conference. Nobody remembers the nondescript conference, because nobody was growing. Commit to action, commit to goals, and do not let this face-to-face opportunity to talk about teaching and learning move forward without an intentional attempt to add value to the professional you serve.

Tips for Tomorrow and Mindset Shifts

Tips for Tomorrow

- Create or download a Ladder of Inference graphic and keep it on your desk.
- Always script questions for a reflective conference.
- Create a system to monitor your own talk time.
- Ask yourself, "If I had more time face-to-face with my teachers to discuss their instructional practices, philosophy, and professionalism, could I have a more profound impact on the overall health of my school?" If the answer is yes—then change your practices to ensure pre- and post-conferences are not opportunities lost because of time constraints.

Mindset Shifts

- Teachers do not need administrators to "fix" them.
- The worst goal is one never set.
- Great evaluators help teachers find the answers within themselves.
- Reflective conferences should never serve as an autopsy—they must always serve to guide future behavior.

Visit pjcaposey.com for additional
resources to improve and transform schools.

Communicate *for* Teachers, Not *to* Them

"The leader must be able to share knowledge and ideas to transmit a sense of urgency and enthusiasm to others. If a leader can't get a message across clearly and motivate others to act on it, then having a message doesn't even matter."

Gilbert Amelio

This year my family moved. We moved less than two miles down the road into a beautiful new house in which we hope to stay for the foreseeable future. I had not moved in several years and, quite honestly, forgot just how stressful, exhausting, and demanding the process can be. In the midst of the move on a warm Friday in July, the expected micro-arguments flared between my better half and me, usually stemming from the re-movement (and re-movement and re-movement) of large, heavy pieces of furniture. By micro-arguments I mean harsh glances, mild retorts of "really" or "come on." Simply put, these were not noticeable yelling matches. These were more of the subtle interactions that take place between couples every single day.

When we were about two-thirds of the way complete with the physical move, a friend, colleague, and mentor of mine who was helping simply said to me as we struggled to move a large dresser up the stairs, "Sometimes the best thing you can do is to be a good husband and just listen." I did not respond and continued to work on backpedaling up the spiraled staircase that seemed much more appealing when shopping for houses as opposed to moving into one. For the next few minutes, as boxes were being moved from one room to other, I continued to think about what my friend had told me. First and foremost, he was right. In the midst of moving thousands of pounds of furniture, was it worth an argument on this day, which should be celebrated, to move a few hundred pounds of furniture a few more feet? Of course it was not. I adjusted my attitude and the remainder of the day went great.

I continued to think about this interaction. The one sentence that was spoken to me, unprovoked, had a drastic impact on my behavior and very likely impacted the experience of everyone else I was around that day. Given that I was already in an iteration of this book, I continued to think about the impact this feedback had on my behavior. In essence, this one sentence did exactly what an effective performance evaluation tries to accomplish, but far too often, with much less success. Why?

EFFECTIVE FEEDBACK STRATEGIES

In May of 2015, transformative educator Grant Wiggins passed away at the age of sixty-four. Wiggins was best known for his work in constructing and popularizing the Understanding by Design lesson planning model that is widely used throughout the world. Wiggins's impact on education extended far beyond that singular contribution, however, as he wrote extensively on a variety of topics. Much of what will be communicated below regarding effective communication strategies is inspired by his work and his tireless efforts to improve our profession.

Goal Referenced

For information to become feedback, it must be aligned to the goals of the person receiving the information. Think about it: We all receive information all day long; some of it we consider feedback, and some of it we simply consider. This is a complex paradigm to operate from but makes complete sense, once you are able to traverse through the density of the thought. The best way I can describe this is through what I refer to as "the hug."

As educators, we have given an innumerable number of speeches to students, parents, and other staff members. Some of the talks are impromptu, and others we have prepared in our minds for days or weeks before the words roll off of our tongues. When we get done with the talk and the subject of the talk walks away, we sometimes congratulate ourselves on a job well done, and other times we simply wonder if that was the talk that was going to take hold and really help someone change direction. Then, five years later, while in line at the grocery store or waiting for a cab, someone who looks familiar but whom you do not quite recognize comes up and gives you a hug. Their first question goes something like, "Mr. C, do you remember me?" As your mind races through a mental rolodex of the thousands of kids you served, the follow-up generally goes, "Remember the one time you said to me . . . it really made a difference. Thank you."

This is the best professional feeling in the world—better than a raise, a standing ovation after a speech, or a compliment on a piece of writing. This is why we do the work we do. For me, I have literally never explicitly remembered the speech or the comment the student shares with me. And it is never one of the great speeches I had planned for weeks.

So, what does this have to do with goal-referenced feedback and the transference of information becoming feedback? Information provided, no matter how eloquently or intelligently, becomes feedback for someone when it helps them. It is about the receiver, not the provider. For the evaluation process to be meaningful and for it to truly impact the professional performance of the teachers administrators serve, it must connect with where the teacher wants to go next. Said simply, if the evaluator gives great directions to travel from Chicago to San Antonio but the teacher wants to travel from Chicago to Des Moines, the directions provided will be dismissed almost instantly.

Information becomes feedback when (in the case of evaluation) the evaluator is able to connect the information provided with a known and agreed upon goal or next step.

Tangible and Transparent

Feedback must mean something—and for it to be effective, it must mean exactly the same thing to the deliverer and to the receiver. For example, both in written evaluations and in observation conferences, student engagement is often discussed. A comment such as, "I would like to see work on engaging students more in the lesson," is not uncommon. The issue is, what exactly does that mean? This always makes me think about the Rick Stiggins quote, "Students can hit any target that they can see and that is not moving" (Stiggins, Arter, Chappuis, & Chappuis, 2004, p. 57). Great feedback does just that—provides a clear target and is firm.

Below are just a few ways the comment about increasing student engagement could possibly be improved. Please note that feedback does not have to exist in the form of a statement. Feedback posed as a question, as discussed in the previous chapter, is often advised to promote teacher ownership of the areas for potential growth:

- Compliance is when kids are doing what we tell them to do and not disrupting the educational process; engagement is when they are using their brains to process through material. Some strategies to increase student engagement are to ask more open-ended questions, allow more time for student collaboration on complex issues, and focus on trying to have every assignment or task reach Levels 4, 5, or 6 of Bloom's Taxonomy.
- Observing your classroom, I could not tell if the kids were engaged or simply copying notes down. Could you tell the difference? How? Could

you explain to me how someone could be doing exactly what you tell her to do and still not be engaged in the lesson? I just want to make sure we are speaking the same language . . .

- What strategies do you prefer to use to increase student engagement, if you perceive students are simply going through the motions? How do you decide when to employ them?

Actionable

Actionable feedback dovetails nicely with the desire for more data-based feedback than in past generations of evaluation commentary. For instance, commentary such as, "Too few questions were asked and most of the time they went without answers—this needs to improve," does not provide anything actionable to the teacher. It allows them to know that questioning needs to improve, but beyond that the feedback is hollow. The same scenario could be observed and an evaluator could provide this varying type of feedback that better meets the needs of the teacher.

> Throughout the entirety of the fifty-two-minute class, the teacher asked five questions. Of those five questions, only one asked for student opinion or allowed for students to respond to something that did not have a correct answer. Two of the questions went without answer for approximately five seconds before the teacher answered the questions himself. Moving forward, make it a goal to ask at least ten questions per class, and at least half of those should be higher order in nature. If students struggle to reply, call on a non-volunteer and be prepared to ask probing questions to eventually scaffold back up to the original question. An example of this would be if the original question were, what motivated the United States to fight in World War II? You could scaffold questions prepared as in the following:
>
> - What things typically lead a country to war?
> - What had taken place in our country to make people angry at other countries?
> - Do you remember whom the United States was fighting in WWII? Had they done anything to provoke the United States?

This feedback provides explicit suggestions that allow someone to change their behavior to meet the demands necessary to execute their next stage of professional growth.

User-Friendly

There are times as educators when we wish we could take the educator hat off and just be a parent or bystander, but most of us cannot complete this task successfully.

This happened for me recently, when I was sitting outside, returning emails, and watching my son's soccer practice. My son, who is nine, is fortunate to have an exceptionally competent and caring coach. During one particular practice toward the beginning of the year, however, the nine-year-olds were acting like, well, nine-year-olds. I started to pay attention to what was taking place. Coach called them over, knelt so he was at their level, and in a very calm voice, proceeded to give them a handful of directions. The directions he gave were multistep and used technical language, and the well-intentioned nine-year-olds glossed over almost immediately.

The young soccer players returned to the field to begin practice again, and the next drill was a disaster. Certain players remembered steps one and two, others none at all, and some simply walked around confused. The issue was that the information provided was not user-friendly. While the directions were delivered in an appropriate manner, were all technically sound and correct instructions, and were goal based and actionable, the feedback being provided failed to cause any change. It failed to cause change because it was too complex (think edu-jargon) and there was too much to digest at once.

User-friendly feedback focuses on providing information that the recipient can use. That means the information must meet them where they currently are, and assumptions about prior knowledge need to be tossed aside. Additionally, the best feedback is usually very focused. Great coaches and leaders focus on the one or two things that if improved will have the most significant impact. This is why it is important for evaluators to understand the crosswalk between best practice and the evaluation frameworks as described in an earlier chapter.

Timely

Timely feedback is important at all levels of education. Communication issues often arise when communication lags from principal to teacher, from teacher to student, and in many other cases in the educational environment as well. The number one rule for evaluators and the timeliness of feedback is to remember that leaders get the behaviors they model and they tolerate. If as a principal you believe it is fine for students to receive feedback on writing ten days later, then treat the teacher in the same manner. If you believe that is too long between the action and the feedback provided, then model the behavior that you wish to see from your teachers.

Two other tips for ensuring your feedback is provided in a timely manner include using the technology tools available to you. There are a plethora of different software platforms that attempt to make the evaluation process less cumbersome and time consuming. Additionally, please make sure to not mistake timely feedback with immediate feedback. While in some cases immediate feedback is preferred, in others, it may not be the best course of action. Remember that trying to have rationale conversation with someone who is reacting to a situation emotionally is almost impossible. Be aware of this fact and (if possible) mold your communication schedule to best align with the outcomes you desire.

Ongoing

This is a small section of the book, but I am not sure there could be a more important section. To continue to make the connection between teacher communication with students and principal communication with teachers is critical. If teachers only provided feedback to students once or twice—even four times per year on their overall performance—we would consider that educational malpractice. However, this is the same support we often provide teachers. I am not here to tell you an exact amount of times you need to observe someone teaching and provide feedback to be effective, because there are too many variables to consider. For instance—does a peer-to-peer observation process exist, or do instructional coaches help support teachers?—are two quick examples. The bottom line is that, for feedback to be meaningful, it first has to be meaningful and important to the person delivering the information. If the information provided is not ongoing, it demonstrates a lack of mutual ownership of future growth, and the principal-teacher feedback process becomes summative in nature instead of formative.

Consistent

Feedback consistency in terms of evaluation manifests itself in three particular ways. First, tone and tenor provided by the evaluator: If the mood of the evaluator is able to be discerned either in a face-to-face meeting or in the written feedback provided, it serves to erode trust in the relationship. This is also a large factor when administrators become short on time—particularly surrounding whatever "due date" is established for evaluations by a district, region, or state. In my review of evaluations as a service to districts, the amount and quality of feedback tend to decrease significantly as a due date looms. The focus shifts from growth to "getting it done."

An additional concern for consistency exists when multiple evaluators, principals, coaches, and so forth, all provide varying feedback in varying ways. There is a desire to increase inter-rater reliability in every situation (think about multiple teachers using the same rubric but scoring it differently), but this goal is of even higher necessity during the evaluation process. If one observer is noted as harsh and critical and another as easy and lax, the entire system implodes upon itself. This form of consistency does not refer to the interpretation of the framework; it refers only to the communication styles of the observers.

The area that needs consistency is in the interpretation of the framework being used. Without clarity on this issue, the entire process becomes muddled for teachers. I liken it to having a curfew of "when it gets dark" for a child during the summer. If Mom interprets that as sunset and Dad interprets this as meaning when it is completely dark outside, a child has no chance to win. If they come in when Mom wants, but Dad is in charge that night, they lose out on playtime. If they come in when Dad wants but Mom is in charge, the child would get in trouble.

This is what happens when the same language gets interpreted differently or enforced differently by different people—the person who loses is the teacher, since the feedback provided is always very difficult to trust.

Tips for Tomorrow and Mindset Shifts

Tips for Tomorrow

- Provide three pieces of feedback each day designed to help others.
- Review five past evaluations, and self-identify commonly used feedback that does not say anything of value to the teacher.
- Touch base with three teachers evaluated in the last semester to gauge their progress on items identified as potential areas of growth.
- Make a sign to hang in your office that reminds you to provide user-friendly feedback and not "edu-jargon."

Mindset Shifts

- How you say things to people is more important than what you say.
- Schedules match priorities: How big of a priority have you made providing timely feedback to your teachers?
- We have the ability to have an incredible influence on others—use this influence wisely.
- Information only becomes feedback when it helps others move closer to their goals.

Visit pjcaposey.com for additional
resources to improve and transform schools.

Personalized Professional Development: Mutually Own Future Growth

"Change is hard because people overestimate the value of what they have—and underestimate the value of what they may gain by giving that up."

James Belasco and Ralph Stayer

If a teacher is under your supervision for multiple years and is still struggling, that is as much a condemnation of the practice of building leaders as it is the individual teacher. Principals and superintendents like to discuss their primary role as that of an instructional leader. If those hired to directly service our students (teachers) are stagnant in their progress and thus kids are not receiving an incredible and ever-improving product, the accountability should start at the very top of the organization. In schools where principals are true instructional leaders, the evaluation process is not simply an annual or biannual event to assess someone's value to the organization. The evaluation is a systematic process to monitor teacher performance and to benchmark their growth in their personal journey. Additionally, the data and conversations uncovered throughout the process serve to directly fuel the next steps of teacher growth.

While the above paragraph may make sense from a philosophical perspective, it is not often what is taking place. I serve as a superintendent in the state of Illinois. In our state, if someone is rated *needs improvement*, we are compelled by school code to implement a professional development plan and to reevaluate the teacher the subsequent year to see if the plan served to improve teacher performance. This is not particularly unique or innovative, and most states have something similar set in place. This makes perfect sense—if someone's performance is not where you want it, you collaboratively create a plan to address growth areas, execute the plan, and re-check. This is a manifestation of a typical continuous improvement cycle.

Hold on a second—this is not an overall win for us as a profession, however. I have spoken to over thirty groups of principals in the state of Illinois on creating a more meaningful evaluation process. I ask the question, is proficient practice from our teachers good enough for our kids? Almost universally, people respond that practice is very good, and we would be happy to have all teachers there, but it is not elite. I think we would agree that we want the best possible teachers working with our kids. I follow that up by asking how many proficient (or whatever label your state or district gives) teachers received professional development plans. The answer is almost universally that nobody does so.

This is a huge contradiction between the game we talk and the effort we put into the evaluation process. We say that we are instructional leaders. We say that there is nothing more critical than helping our teachers get better. We say that we believe a formalized plan for professional growth is likely to deliver results. Then, we only spend the time and energy to create such a plan with those who are really struggling and do nothing formal for those who range between fine, good, great, and even elite. Simply put, most school leaders and school districts do nothing to commit to mutually owning the growth of teachers that are performing at or above average. The result for kids—a whole lot of the status quo.

Establishing a Personalized Professional Development Plan for Teachers

Most people do not really need convincing that a PD (professional development) plan for teachers is a good thing. The issue becomes the time involved, the process to develop a plan, and the plan for accountability. There is a struggle—in this case with the WHAT and the HOW but not the WHY. The first step to demystifying this process is understanding how to create an effective plan.

Components of an Effective Plan

Effective plans have six components. This is not just a blueprint or template for an effective PD plan; this is a blueprint or template for any plan. The six components are a goal, activities, timelines, deliverables, a measure of success, and a person to be held responsible for each activity. Visually, a PD plan would take the format shown in the following figure (Figure 9.1).

Figure 9.1 Professional Development Plan Template

			GOAL		
Current Reality	Activity	To be completed by: (date)	Deliverable	Person responsible for this activity	Measure of success

Goal

Establishing the goal, particularly for a PD plan, is often the trickiest part of the entire process. Often, a teacher will think that the goal is simply to achieve a higher rating. And while a higher rating will hopefully occur as a result of accomplishing the goal, the intent of growing as a professional educator should never be to earn a higher performance evaluation rating. The intent should be to improve upon professional practice to better serve kids. As the leader of the conversation, the evaluator must be dogged in having the teacher commit to goals that revolve around student behavior, which can be measured objectively.

My belief is the manner in which to best explain this process is to walk through what a potential conversation around a PD plan may look like. (Evaluator will be abbreviated E and teacher will be abbreviated T.)

E: What do you think one of your goal areas should be?

T: I think I should focus on questioning. It is one of the two areas where I received a lower rating.

E: That is perfect; I would have suggested questioning as well. What do you have in mind for a goal?

T: Well, I guess my goal is to be *proficient* when it comes to asking students questions.

E: I would like you to think about how we can make this change about driving the performance of kids, not just impacting your evaluation.

T: I am not sure what you mean.

E: OK, let me walk you through a few questions.

T: OK.

E: Why do you want to get better at asking questions?—only thinking about kids, not yourself.

T: Well, I think the kids would engage more if I asked more or better questions.

E: Why do you think they would engage more?

T: Sometimes it feels like the more I am talking the less they are engaged.

E: So, if I am understanding, what you are saying is that you want to increase student engagement by improving how you ask questions?

T: Yes.

E: So, how can we tell if whatever we plan on doing is actually working?

T: Well, I think if kids talk more, that is a first step, and second would be if they were more engaged.

E: How could we tell if they are more engaged?

T: I would probably have to write fewer referrals, and kids would probably do better on their tests.

E: Do you realize that you have created three different goals and three different ways we can measure your progress, all based on wanting to improve your questioning?

T: So, I could measure my progress how?

E: You could measure how much you talk compared to how much students talk, you could measure how many referrals you write compared to how many you wrote last semester, and you can measure student achievement on assessments you give.

This may be an over-simplification of the process, but I think it tells the story. If you ask why enough times, you almost always arrive at something that involves kids and can be measured. It is important to remember that although we are setting measureable goals for the sake of the PD plan, the reward is in the journey (hopefully), not only in the outcome. To further explain, if somebody goes through the steps you provide and grows tremendously as a teacher but does not reach the benchmark set that should in no way negatively impact their next performance evaluation rating.

Activity

The activity is what the teacher is going to do to help achieve their goal. In the above scenario, the theme of the goal is to improve questioning. Activities toward this end are almost limitless. The activities can be as simple as scripting five questions before each class that the teacher commits to asking to as complex as attending a national conference and everything in between. One thing we are not lacking in education is tips and ideas on how to improve in a specific area. Ideas and resources range from heavily researched to video guides made by novice teachers and anything in between. When beginning to construct a plan, it always seems that the activities are the most important element to consider. In actuality, the most important aspect is following a continuous improvement cycle. There are many to choose from. My favorite is Plan, Do, Check, Act (PDCA). The reality is that most targeted personal PD plans yield results. The role of the evaluator is to monitor progress to ensure progress is taking place.

Timelines

Timelines are self-explanatory, but they are an essential part of the plan. Deadlines drive action. They also create simple markers for communication and check-ins between evaluator and teacher. A plan without a deadline is simply a concept, not a course of action. Deadlines also allow for a scaffolding of the plan. If there are areas more complex than others, a well-devised plan with staggered deadlines allows for growth to occur before potentially overwhelming a teacher who you are attempting to support.

Person Accountable

This is an area that is scary for evaluators. If this process leads to the evaluator doing a tremendous amount of work, the job simply becomes too big for any one person to handle. If the process leads to the teacher engaging in several different professional activities to help them grow, the job may become too pressure-filled, and the job of teaching may be diminished. This type of *apparent* lose-lose is what helps propel many leaders into inaction. This does not have to be, nor should it be, the situation.

Whenever I am working with someone and I have the guttural instinct to do some of the work for them, I always ask myself if I think Hall of Fame coach of Duke University, Mike Krzyzewski (NCAA men's basketball's winningest coach), takes layups at practice. When you state it like that, it sounds like nonsense. Of course a seventy-year-old coach would not be working on his fundamentals at practice. Instead, he would be leading and coaching. The players would be putting in the work necessary in order to improve. Great principals do not shoot layups for their teachers—they let them work, get better, and earn the dividends that come from their own personal effort.

It is not uncommon to find yourself wondering how much work is too much work to ask someone to complete to fuel his or her own professional development. A mentor of mine often says there are only two types of people in this world—those you have to tell to go faster and those you have to tell to slow down. Working in a culture where the predominant worry is whether or not you are pushing too hard is not a healthy environment for change or progress. While it is certainly true that it is possible to overwork people, it is also possible to not be demanding enough. The difficult part of our jobs is that we work every day with children, and not pushing people to be their best directly impacts kids.

So, while no simple answer exists that tells us exactly how hard and how fast to push, because everyone is an individual, the one absolute is that nobody was hired to maintain the status quo. Growth and change are not optional in successful schools. Great leaders are able to find the sweet spot for moving people forward. For me, the sweet spot is somewhere between comfortable and paralyzed by stress. To quote Thoreau, "The price of anything is the amount of life you exchange for it" (n.d.), and nothing better describes the journey to professional excellence. Great leaders find a way to make their team comfortably uncomfortable. Great teams are always moving forward, faster than most thought possible, but never reckless in direction or with the hearts of the people on the journey. The bottom line is that most leaders push far too soft rather than too hard. As leaders we must overcome the fear of pushing too hard to achieve truly uncommon growth and uncommon results.

Measure of Success

Many have gone on life-altering fitness journeys, and for those who have not, most of us have at least been on a diet before. Can you imagine going on a diet or a fitness program where you did not weigh in, take measurements, or measure success in some way? It seems counter-intuitive to think that anyone just wings it and assumes what they are trying is working when it comes to health and fitness. This mentality, however, is pervasive in the school setting.

In education, we have a bad habit of loving data that affirms our predispositions, and we tend to reject data that exposes ideas contrary to what we previously held. As a result, we struggle to find metrics for which we are willing to hold ourselves accountable. The issue is often that every measure is imperfect in education. This imperfection does not forgive us the responsibility of working toward an end and measuring our progress forward. This struggle is evident in many areas of schooling but profoundly present when creating a PD plan with a teacher.

For instance, someone is going to read *Blended Learning in Action* by Tucker, Wycoff, and Green as part of the plan to help them accomplish a goal of increasing student achievement by better personalizing learning. While this one activity supports the overarching goal, it too should have a metric of success. When first implementing PD plans, such measures often are compliance measures. For instance, Mr. Morris will finish the book by August of next year. While this is the purpose of the activity, it would not be an adequate measure of success. A measure of success would be something along the lines of, Mr. Morris will identify two strategies he would like to implement from the book and invite the evaluator in to see them in practice by (insert random date). Earlier in the chapter, we talked about the student-driven nature of the overall goal—and while each activity's goal should align with the overall process, the measure of success does not need to be as specific or driven directly by student outcomes.

WHAT HAPPENS IF I AM NOT AN EXPERT IN THIS AREA?

One of the most common questions I receive from principals when trying to convince them a PD plan for every professional is vital to continuous school improvement is one raised directly out of lack of confidence. Principals have a hard time creating a thorough plan if they do not believe they are experts in the field or if in the particular area the teacher has the most potential professional growth. The answer to this is simple—treat your teachers the way you would want them to treat their students, particularly if that student was your child. No administrator would accept the rationale that a teacher was not going to work on helping a student address a deficiency because the teacher was not an expert in that area. Instead, they would tell the teacher to consult peers, use social networks to connect with exemplars, and work with the student to collaboratively find the answer and grow. These are precisely the steps an evaluator should take when constructing a plan in an area where they are not abundantly confident.

Consult Peers

There is no doubt that at times being a principal can be a lonely existence. In today's educational landscape, however, principals have nobody but themselves to blame if they feel isolated. Connecting with peers in one's geographic area is supported through professional meetings, cooperatives for specialized services, and simple networking. Additionally, most professional organizations have listserves, which act as a safe space for well-intentioned professionals to interact and gain expertise. If a teacher needs help with effective questioning strategies, a failure to engage and connect with local peers is generally born out of insecurity and/or hubris and not lack of opportunity. I encourage all administrators to not forfeit the opportunity to impact change for your teachers (and thereby your students) out of a personal fear of asking for help.

Use Social Networks and Technology Tools for Support

If typical interaction with your peers is something that you are not comfortable with or you dislike for any number of reasons, many new options have emerged in the past two decades. For instance, simply Googling "sample growth plan to increase student engagement" literally yields millions of potential leads. This reach can be amplified and made more personalized if you are connected via social media. Personally, I have found no greater free professional development than what I have been exposed to on Twitter (where you can find me @MCUSDSupe).

I have been able to connect personally with the greatest educational minds of our time and exchange ideas, steal resources, and even engage in healthy discourse. Twitter, when used appropriately, is like the world's most crowded teachers' lounge, filled with energetic, passionate, and well-intentioned teachers. It makes little sense, if you know that exists, to not expose yourself to the incredible ideas and dialogue that is organically taking place twenty-four hours a day, seven days a week.

Problem Solve Together

I saved my preferred solution for last. Admitting that you are not the foremost expert to someone you lead is not a sign of weakness. Instead, it is a sign of strength. In addition to the humility it shows to admit you are not educationally omniscient, the joint resource-finding mission can lead to a better relationship with the person you are walking down this path with. Remember, this is ultimately their growth plan, not yours. The greater the ownership of the plan by the teacher, starting with Stage 1, the better.

Tips for Tomorrow and Mindset Shifts

Tips for Tomorrow

- Agree upon a PD plan template and follow it.
- Create a timeline for implementation and philosophy for when and how to create PD plans.
- Create overall growth goals for teachers that always are reliant on student outcomes, not teacher effort.

Mindset Shifts

- Forgive yourself for not knowing everything and commit to using supplemental tools.
- Teacher effort is part of the plan; increased student performance is the desired outcome.
- PD plans do not have to take an enormous amount of principal time.
- Proficient practice is to be commended, but it cannot be good enough if you want to have an elite school. Proficient teachers need help too.

Visit pjcaposey.com for additional
resources to improve and transform schools.

Conclusion (and a
Note to Superintendents)

"There's a big difference between showing interest and really taking interest."

Michael P. Nichols

Districts can look at teacher evaluation in one of two ways, either as a district's best, most systematic opportunity to influence the growth of teachers or as a process that simply assesses a teacher's value to the organization. Truth be told, the process—out of necessity—needs to function as a little of both.

Using EXTREMELY conservative time estimates, an administrator with just fifteen teachers under their direct supervision will spend over sixty hours of the school year on the evaluation process. When I talk to my principals and principals I work with in other districts, I consistently hear how time intensive the process is and how much stress and angst it causes for our building leaders. Conversely, when teaching graduate courses, my discussions with FUTURE building leaders around the topic of evaluation have been fascinating. In my last cohort of students, I asked how many of them found the evaluation process meaningful. The answer was ZERO.

We have a major issue in our schools that we seem to be systematically ignoring as superintendents. We have outstanding rubrics to choose from, whether you prefer Marzano or Danielson or a hybrid model. Most states have statutory guidance on how to implement a data-based segment of teacher evaluation. Principals have generally received quality training to help them learn the selected evaluation instrument, and countless other state-mandated trainings have been completed surrounding the topic of evaluation.

The question for each of you and for each of us to answer is simple—has all of that work made any difference? Study after study shows that the single greatest determinant in the success of a school is the quality of its teachers. Said simply, the quality of a school system simply cannot exceed the quality of its teachers.

The question becomes singly, is your teacher evaluation system making a difference? Is your system helping teachers grow from their Point A to their Point B? My honest opinion after working with a multitude of districts and school administrators is that you cannot honestly answer these massively important questions.

We cannot answer those questions because we do not normally know what is taking place during this process. Think about it—we would all label ourselves instructional leaders, but during the one opportunity we have as an organization to systematically impact teacher growth, we are usually completely void of self-reflection and critical analysis of our own performance. This book is designed to help us not only grow as evaluators but also learn what questions we should be asking of ourselves to help each other continue to grow in this role.

The bottom line and the biggest unspoken truth in educational leadership is this—there simply is no perfect system. If there was, we would all employ it, close every achievement gap, and reach levels of unprecedented success in every district. This simply does not happen. Almost everything we try to improve our schools *can* work. The question is, does it work well enough and quick enough? When it comes to evaluation, remember that your system is perfectly aligned to get the results currently being produced. And unless these results indicate an ever-improving and fundamental transformation of the instructional practices in your building or district, the results are probably not ideal. Thus, the only way we improve our educational systems and practices is to improve the people with them. That is our charge. That is my impassioned plea. That is my hope. I hope this book helps us help each other grow and become amazing at serving the children so dependent upon us.

Additional Resources for School Leaders to Examine	
Software to support the evaluation process	www.insightadvance.com https://www.evaluwise.org/ https://www.standardforsuccess.com/sfs/ http://www.goteachpoint.com/ https://www.t-eval.com/ https://www.frontlineeducation.com/Insights/teachscape_login.html
Resources to continue to read about evaluation and providing better feedback—inclusive of great ideas and suggestions for improvement	http://k12education.gatesfoundation.org/resource/better-feedback-for-better-teaching-a-practical-guide-to-improving-classroom-observations/ http://www.ascd.org/publications/educational-leadership/sept12/vol70/num01/Seven-Keys-to-Effective-Feedback.aspx https://www.engageny.org/

A Note to Superintendents

With awareness comes responsibility. In my time as a superintendent, I can think of no phrase that has better explained any success that I have had. This phrase has also led me down stressful, time-consuming roads that would have been "easier" left in the dark. As district leaders, we have not been hired to do what is easy—we have been hired to do what is best for kids.

If you have read this book, I hope that (at minimum) you have several questions about how the evaluation process really works in your district. I am confident that the vast majority of schools and districts have a set policy and procedures that are followed to the letter of law, school code, or internal regulations. That, however, is not what I believe superintendents need to be strongly considering. Instead, I am hoping that each of you take away from this book the question of whether your system for evaluations satisfactorily meets the purpose of systematically improving the performance of every teacher in your district.

The question posed is massive, and if the answer is not a strong "yes," then much work is left in front of each of us. That feeling is awareness. With this awareness comes responsibility, and the challenge of transforming a system such as this is immense. Below are five quick strategies that are within the purview of district-level executive administration that will directly lead to evaluation system improvements and help superintendents move from absent to profoundly present during the teacher evaluation process. While these suggestions do require some investment of time and resources—if our schedules and budgets match our priorities, then this seems like a no-brainer.

Read Your Evaluations

I cannot think of a simpler, yet more profound shift in how most districts conduct the business of evaluation. In my second year as a superintendent, I spent ninety hours of our winter break reading every line of every evaluation completed over the last two years in my district. I learned more about my principals and our teachers than I had learned in my previous years in the district. I found gaps in performance and perception, evaluation themes, some instances of wonderful practice, and some practices that made me cringe. If you do not have ninety hours—hire someone internally or externally to complete an analysis and provide you feedback so that you may target practices that need improvement.

Observe Evaluations

I hope that as a profession, superintendents are taking the time to evaluate our principals. Remember, leaders get the behaviors they model and tolerate. If you do not model that evaluation is a rigorous and important process centered on growth, it will be hard to convince your principals that they need to treat it as such with their teachers. One thing that the evaluation process for principals is seemingly lacking is the opportunity for an observation that is truly meaningful. I encourage you to take the time to sit in on a pre-conference, observation, and post-observation. This time commitment demonstrates an investment in the process and the growth of both principals and teachers. More tangibly, this first-hand experience helps provide insight to better coach your principals, gives a glimpse of life in the trenches, and demonstrates to your teachers that you are not disconnected from their reality.

Leverage the Pre-conference

There is not a single process in schools that I find as under-leveraged as the pre-conference. Typical pre-conferences are a waste of time. Asking teachers to answer questions you already asked them to answer in writing or asking them to tell you what you will see is literally pointless. Continually asking WHAT questions, like "what will I see?" as opposed to WHY and HOW questions, such as, "how did you decide to teach it that way?" and "why do you think that is the best pedagogical approach?" We cannot help people grow with *what* questions. This is examined in detail in an earlier chapter, but this is an avenue of practice a superintendent and executive leadership can directly impact or control, and thus it is included in this chapter as well.

Focus on Your Principals

This concept was reinforced through professional development provided by IASA's Rich Voltz. If you are using Danielson, there is so much to focus on it becomes hard to focus. Often, the forest cannot be seen through the trees. A strong focus on student engagement—true engagement in critical thought, not simply compliance—will lead to significant growth. Becoming an expert in all areas of either of the popular evaluation frameworks can seem simply overwhelming. Becoming a master of one is a much more palatable challenge for our principals. Providing this guidance and making the process less intimidating is a key step to moving evaluations forward.

Create a System

As superintendent, you simply cannot DO every teacher evaluation. That said, there is a responsibility to lead the process. Creating a system, providing professional development, and having some type of principal accountability measure *should* be a requisite part of our job. We have the duty to support our principals through this process. Change occurs in one of two ways. One, we can think our way into a new way of behaving, or two, we can behave our way into a new of thinking. As intellectuals and leaders, there can be significant debate as to which modality is the most effective. That is why I suggest that, as leaders, we attempt to influence change simultaneously through both strategies. Thereby, creating firm protocols and expectations to change behavior will help to, in time, change the way people think about the evaluation process.

Superintendents must not just talk a good game about being instructional leaders—they must commit time and resources to truly leading this very important process.

        Visit pjcaposey.com for additional
resources to improve and transform schools.

Resource

Suggestions-for-Improvement Bank

| | Visit pjcaposey.com for links to all resources mentioned in this bank. |

Topic, Subject, Components	Potential Suggestions for Improvement to Be Provided to the Teacher

Content mastery and pedagogy	• Work to not impose adult teaching preferences that may not align to how children think at given times
	
	Resource #1: Piaget's Stages
	
	• Work to understand brain development and stages of development of students at given ages
	
	Resource #2: What's the Brain Got to Do With It? 10 Brain Facts for Educators
	
	• Demonstrate mastery of content and truly appear to drive instruction instead of being the facilitator of a textbook or canned curriculum
	• Use data to drive what instructional strategy you use to deliver what content—do not fall into routines or ruts
	• The ability of a teacher to provide clear goals to begin any unit is essential. It demonstrates the teacher knows what is important and to be valued so that the students may know the same.
	
	Resource #3: Learning Outcomes
	
	• Intentionally work to develop content knowledge or pedagogical skill through your choice of the following
	  ○ Online learning
	  ○ Graduate courses
	  ○ Conferences
	  ○ Articles, books, etc.

(Continued)

(Continued)

Topic, Subject, Components	Potential Suggestions for Improvement to Be Provided to the Teacher
Data, knowledge of students, stage of development	• Work so that students understand their own data and set ambitious, yet reasonable goals for themselves **Resource #4: Setting Goals: Who, Why, How?** • Give a survey and disaggregate results based on learning preferences, heritage, and student assessment of current skill at the beginning of semester or year **Resource #5: A Questionnaire for Students on the First Day of School** • Work to not impose adult teaching preferences that may not align to how children think at given times • Work to understand brain development and stages of development of students at given ages **Resource #6: A Quick Guide to the Middle School Brain** • Substantial student data are needed to determine the type and intensity of necessary intervention—work to gather such information for all students • Note that students in intervention should be expected to grow more than one year in that time frame given the additional time and intensity of service **Resource #7: The Next Generation of Response to Intervention**
Instructional outcomes	• Set a core goal for each unit • Use student contracts to outline specific goals **Resource #8: Grades 6-8 Goal Setting** • Employ *true* essential questions **Resource #9: Essential Questions** • Have students copy objectives each day and report out on their progress toward them sporadically during the unit • Have students commit to writing their expectation for performance against each stated outcome prior to a unit beginning **Resource #10: Accelerate Student Achievement for All by Increasing Student Self-Assessment and Expectations** • Clearly articulate learning outcomes daily and then measure student progress toward them. Once data is collected, make sure to adjust instruction, but leave instructional objectives firm • The teacher providing clear direction as to where student learning will lead increases student achievement

Topic, Subject, Components	Potential Suggestions for Improvement to Be Provided to the Teacher
Instructional outcomes (continued)	• Plan for differentiation—do not just react. Create multiple pathways to success for each essential outcome and continue to build tools to ensure you can serve all learners **Resource #11: Planning for Differentiation** • Take time to learn what differentiation truly means on a deeper level. **Resource #12: Carol Tomlinson Presentation**
Understanding available resources	• Ensure that as a teacher you know all potential support systems available to a student in your district to provide intervention or enrichment • Be able to articulate how you matched resources to student skill level instead of simply accepting what was in the classroom **Resource #13: Differentiating the Content** • Create a log (electronic preferred) of available resources for all students • Identify one person outside of the school setting you can learn from and work with to better serve your students • Work to find mentors to match students with outside of the school environment. These can be professional mentors or simply someone to read with and to help with homework **Resource #14: The ABCs of School-Based Mentoring**
Coherent instruction, grouping plans, lesson planning	• Group students using a variety of criteria (academic data, common interest, past experience, introvert/extrovert) • Vary group sizes, roles within the group, and objective of the group setting **Resource #15: Instruction Based on Cooperative Learning** • Design work around positive interdependence, group processing, social skills, promoting face-to-face interaction, and understanding having responsibility to yourself and to the group **Resource #16: Positive Interdependence, Individual Accountability, Promotive Interaction: Three Pillars of Cooperative Learning** • Two quick examples are QAR and Think, Pair, Share **Resource #17: Question Answer Relationship: Teaching Children Where to Seek Answers to Questions**

(Continued)

(Continued)

Topic, Subject, Components	Potential Suggestions for Improvement to Be Provided to the Teacher
(continued) Coherent instructions, grouping plans, lesson planning	• Clear connections and goals are established linking their learning to desired outcomes and other disciplines when appropriate **Resource #18: Aligning the Curriculum** • Remember if you assign something and receive 25 similar products it was a recipe, not a project • Implement a tried and true lesson planning system or template such as Understanding by Design **Resource #19: Making the Most of Understanding by Design: A Summary of Lessons Learned**
Designing assessment	• Feedback should be provided in a timely and *corrective* manner (should inform kids as to how to improve) **Resource #20: POD – Idea Center Notes** • Find ways for student self-assessment to take place where teacher's role is to validate student opinion **Resource #21: The Effects of Self-Assessment on Academic Performance** • Allow for student-led sessions to discuss overall feedback themes and allow for peer to peer teaching to take place based on general findings • Ensure student mastery over criteria being assessed to a point where they can predict their own performance—and have them communicate their expectations in writing • Formative assessment should align directly with both learning objectives and upcoming summative assessments **Resource #22: Assessment Blueprint: Aligning an Assessment to Course Standards, Content, Skills, and Rigor** • Formative assessments are only useful if that data are used to adjust teaching methods and/or provide additional support for struggling students **Resource #23: The Impact of Formative Assessment and Learning Intentions on Student Achievement**
Classroom environment, teacher-student relationships	• Earn trust by showing trust to students **Resource #24: Building Trust With Students** • Students do not care how much know until they know how much you care **Resource #25: Building (and Maintaining) Rapport in the Classroom**

Topic, Subject, Components	Potential Suggestions for Improvement to Be Provided to the Teacher
(continued) Classroom environment, teacher–student relationships	• Provide students with not only an objective, but also the WHY as to its importance and the HOW as to how they will need to show you they understand **Resource #26: Examples of Organizational Why, How, What Strategy** • View your job as creating a roadmap for learning for each child. The child should be able to tell you where they are at along the way (at any given time)
Classroom culture	• Intentionally teach grit **Resource # 27: Perseverance and Grit Can Be Taught** • Personalize recognition for hard work and high-quality performance **Resource #28: Tips for Encouraging Good Attendance in the Classroom Through Incentives and Recognition** • Use PPP (Pause, Prompt, Praise) for students who are struggling or need additional scaffolding **Resource #29: Pause, Prompt, Praise** • Have students keep a weekly log of EFFORT and ACHIEVEMENT—provide feedback • Student expectations for their own performance is a great predictor of actual performance—create an environment and strategies for them to set their own standard which you support them in reaching as opposed to you setting the standard for them **Resource #30: Not All Teaching Practices are Created Equal** • For students to assume ownership of their learning, they must be given certain levels of autonomy and the ability to take risks **Resource #31: Developing Responsible and Autonomous Learners: A Key to Motivating Success** • Teacher provides laser like focus for students as to what needs to be learned, why it is important, and how they can demonstrate mastery
Classroom procedures	• Clear learning intentions apply to routines and classroom based skills as well as essential curricula. Clarity in expectations help to allow students to take ownership of classroom procedures **Resource #32: Managing Classroom Procedures**

(Continued)

(Continued)

Topic, Subject, Components	Potential Suggestions for Improvement to Be Provided to the Teacher
(continued) Classroom procedures	• Take time to teach the desired behavior and then demand it is executed • If you (the teacher) demonstrate how valuable class time is, the students will begin to value it as such as well
Classroom management, student behavior	• Clear, unwavering, equitable behavior expectations are the key to a well-managed class **Resource #33: Frequent Monitoring and Student Recognition Whiteman Elementary School** • Operate from the paradigm that students misbehaving are not doing so to disrespect you, but are acting out based on the crises taking place in other parts of their lives. Do not take it personal **Resource #34: Trauma Informed Approaches to Classroom Management** • Referrals are a part of the management process, however, they indicate that internal (classroom) management processes did not yield the desired results. Referrals mean that student behavior should change—and it should also indicate adult behavior should change
Physical environment	• Remove physical barriers between teacher and students • Spend more time among students than in front of them • Work tirelessly to ensure classroom accessibility for all students—should be a top priority when designing the physical layout of the classroom • Discussions work best when students can see other face-to-face. Given that classroom discussion is a high yield strategy keep that in mind when organizing your room • Add one new technology tool to your repertoire each month **Resource #35: 15 Tech Tool Favorites From ISTE 2016**
Communicating with students; teacher clarity	• Using metaphors and similes intentionally help to provide opportunities for connection for students—do so intentionally and daily • Clearly communicate the learning objectives in a manner students can use to ultimately self-assess their own learning **Resource #36: Writing Measurable Learning Outcomes** • Increase power and presence in speaking by eliminating pauses, Umms, Oks, You Knows, etc. **Resource #37: Verbal Fillers in Public Speaking**

Topic, Subject, Components	Potential Suggestions for Improvement to Be Provided to the Teacher
(continued) Communicating with students; teacher clarity	• Use explicit knowledge of student preferences to tailor individual instruction to their needs (skill deficiency—not learning style). This is particularly useful when working with struggling learners
	Resource #38: Is Learning Styles-Based Instruction Effective?
	• Set a core goal for each unit and each day, and explain why it is important and how students need to be demonstrate their understanding
	Resource #39: Six Strategies to Help Students Cite and Explain Evidence
Questioning and discussion	• Ask students to identify similarities and differences using Venn diagrams and other graphic organizers
	Resource #40: Venn Diagram Lesson
	• Have students use figurative language, metaphors, and similes to explain important concepts
	Resource #41: In a Manner of Speaking: Figurative Language and the Common Core
	• Make use of content frames or semantic feature analysis
	Resource #42: 11 Brilliant Ways To Frame Critical Content: A Complexities Chart
	Resource #43: Semantic Feature Analysis
	• Ask students to predict what would happen if one or two elements of a situation were changed
	Resource #44: Teaching Inference
	• Use the popsicle stick method of calling on students with a redundant system to provide "security" for students
	Resource #45: Popsicle Stick Method
	• Employ Hypothesis Proof note-taking
	Resource #46: Taking Column Notes
	• Employ at least a 5-second wait time after asking questions and NEVER answer your own question
	Resource #47: Wait Time and Education
	• Effective questioning can serve as ongoing formative assessment for the classroom as well as individuals
	Resource #48: Formative Assessment Strategies: Asking Powerful Questions for Greater Student Engagement
	• Question scaffold based on Bloom's taxonomy
	Resource #49: Bloom's Taxonomy

(Continued)

(Continued)

Topic, Subject, Components	Potential Suggestions for Improvement to Be Provided to the Teacher
(continued) Questioning and discussion	• Teaching students the Piagetian stages of development and Bloom's taxonomy explicitly will help students to think through their thinking **Resource #50: Teaching Students Bloom's Taxonomy** • Remember: answering questions is a subtle way to formatively assess—call on non-volunteers • Script 3 to 5 higher order questions for each class period designed to instigate authentic classroom discussion

Student engagement	• All note-taking should involve a student-generated further questions and summarization section
	Resource #51: Introduction to Note-Taking
	
	• Employ graphic organizers—they force students to manipulate content instead of simply regurgitate
	Resource #52: Instructional Strategy Lessons for Educators
	
	• Strategies include:
	  ○ Content Frames
	Resource #53: Content Frame
	
	  ○ Semantic Feature Analysis
	Resource #54: Semantic Feature Analysis
	
	  ○ KWL
	Resource #55: K-W-L (Know, Want to Know, Learned)
	
	  ○ QAR
	Resource #56: Question-Answer Relationship (QAR)
	
	  ○ Hypothesis Proof Note-Taking
	Resource #57: Column Notes
	
	• Formalize a goal-setting process that engages student in a daily self-assessment of their progress toward a goal
	Resource #58: Student Goal Settings on Pinterest
	
	• Script 3 to 5 higher order questions for each class period designed to instigate authentic classroom discussion
	Resource #59: Higher Order Thinking Questions

Assessment, instructional assessment, formative assessment	• Work to ensure that neither you nor a student is ever surprised by a student's performance on an assessment **Resource #60: The Best Value in Formative Assessment by Stephen Chappuis and Jan Chappuis**

Topic, Subject, Components	Potential Suggestions for Improvement to Be Provided to the Teacher
(continued) Assessment, instructional assessment, formative assessment	• Formative assessment should directly tie to summative assessment which should directly tie to Essential Outcomes/Core Standards, etc. **Resource #61: Assessment and the Teaching and Learning Cycle** • Measurement of a lesson's success should be the student progress toward the daily outcome—use a variety of strategies to measure ○ Exit tickets **Resource #62: Exit Tickets: Checking for Understanding** ○ Journal entries **Resource #63: Learning From Formative Assessment by Jennifer Atkinson** ○ Individual whiteboard responses **Resource #64: Classroom Techniques: Formative Assessment by Kelly Goodrich** ○ One minute essay **Resource #65: The One-Minute Paper** ○ Any number of tech-aided survey tools such as Kahoot or Flubaroo **Resource #66: Find a Formative Assessment Tool in Kahoot!** **Resource #67: Google Docs + Flubaroo = Formative Assessment in a Snap** ○ Three Facts and a Fib **Resource #68: 3 Facts & a Fib** ○ My Favorite No • Assessment data—both local and screener should guide intervention programs and SAT referrals **Resource #69: Linking Progress Monitoring Results to Interventions by Jennifer N. Mahdavi and Diane Haager** • Instruction should always change to meet the needs of students who have failed to master content as originally presented **Resource #70: 3 Ways Student Data Can Inform Your Teaching by Rebecca Alber**

(Continued)

(Continued)

Topic, Subject, Components	Potential Suggestions for Improvement to Be Provided to the Teacher
Teacher flexibility, teachable moments	• Have the courage to allow students to stir the conversation and you as the expert can work to highlight teachable moments and reign in off-topic rants **Resource #71: Embracing Teachable Moments by Gabby Ross** • Learning matters more than coverage—always leverage opportunities to deeply engage your students • Work to create lesson plans that allow for adaptation and increased depth of conversation when appropriate • Teacher Excellence and Support System **Resource #72: Possible Strategies to Enhance Instructional Practice**
Reflection	• Great reflection is based on data, not feelings. Formative evaluation should fuel whether or not a teacher found the lesson effective or not **Resource #73: Teaching Strategies: The Value of Self-Reflection by Janelle Cox** • Employ micro-teaching **Resource #74: John Hattie's Top Ten Visible Learning Takeaways—Number Six: Microteaching** ○ Video a lesson to get a better understanding of what actually is taking place during a lesson ○ Work with a cohort of teachers to observe each other and provide thorough feedback and suggestions for improvement • Improvement suggestions provided by the teacher indicate depth of thought and not just more of the same slower, faster, better, etc. **Resource #75: Expanding Our Teaching Repertoire: Why Is It So Important and So Bloody Difficult?**
Record keeping	• Students should have a responsibility in keeping their own records and progress toward stated goals **Resource #76: The Art and Science of Teaching/When Students Track Their Progress by Robert J. Marzano** • Grade books should be updated regularly—falling behind in grading is not appropriate **Resource #77: Seven Keys to Effective Feedback by Grant Wiggins**

Topic, Subject, Components	Potential Suggestions for Improvement to Be Provided to the Teacher
(continued) Record keeping	• Students can be in charge of creating late and missing work folders for students who are not in attendance **Resource #78: The Absent Binder** • Students can update social media and other electronic platforms with learning objectives, notes, and pending assignments **Resource #79: Social Media in the Classroom: 16 Resources for 2015 by Joy Nelson**
Parent communication	• No parent, student, or teacher should ever be surprised by a summative assessment score. Formative assessment should provide information to proactively address student skill deficiencies **Resource #80: Proactive Parent Communication** • Communicate based on the "Fence and 2" method. Anyone on the fence of an A or an F and/or anyone who has rapidly moved two grade values deserves attention—whether positive or negative • Employ student-led communication in all facets, including PTCs **Resource #81: Implementing Student-Led Conferences in Your School by Patti Kinney** • Leverage student technology to your advantage—if you have two minutes at the end of class, have students email their parents a current self-created progress report and CC you on the message

Team mindset, role within the school, participating in a PLC	• A poor district has no leadership, in a good district administration leads, in a great district—teachers lead. We need you. Find something you are passionate about
	
	Resource #82: The Importance of Learning From Other Teacher Leaders
	
	   o Join a pre-existing committee
	   o Drive work in an area you are passionate about
	
	Resource #83: Teaching and Leading from Within: A Courage & Renewal Program for Educators
	
	   o Do not fear anything being too big or too small—if you are interested in brain based learning then start a group, etc.
	• Lead the effort to install a peer to peer observation practice in our schools
	
	Resource #84: Teachers Observing Teachers: A Professional Development Tool for Every School

(Continued)

(Continued)

Topic, Subject, Components	Potential Suggestions for Improvement to Be Provided to the Teacher
(continued) Team mindset, role within the school, participating in a PLC	• Take time to micro-teach mini-lessons with colleagues providing feedback or video your own classroom to provide yourself a different perspective to inform future improvement efforts • **Read**—Join a professional scholarly journal, go online and read educational blogs, or read some literature on education. Knowledge is power. **Resource #85: Professional Development Tips for Teachers by Janelle Cox** • **Participate**—Go to educational conferences or workshops, or attend online seminars. Participation in these types of event will make you a more effective teacher. • **Join a Group**—There are many groups you that you can join, online and off. All of these groups are a great source of information as well as inspiration. You can learn a lot from other professionals who have years of experience. • **Observe Your Peers**—An effective teacher takes the time to observe other teachers. These teachers can be a great source of knowledge for you. You can find a new strategy to teach or behavior management plan to implement. • **Share**—Once you have improved your performance, then you should share your knowledge with others. Contribute to your profession, and others will be thankful.
Professionalism	• Be a champion for those traditionally underserved **Resource #86: Teaching and Classroom Strategies for Homeless and Highly Mobile Students** • Our goal is not equality, our goal is doing what it takes to ensure all kids are successful (equity) **Resource #87: Equity vs. Equality: 6 Steps Toward Equity by Shane Safir** • Do not allow work in teams, grade levels, or PLC to devolve into anything outside of talk that best meets the needs of our students **Resource #88: Every School Has One: Principals Share Tips For Working With Negative People**

References

Adams, G., Danielson, C., Moilanen, G., & Association for Supervision and Curriculum Development. (2009). *Enhancing professional practice: A framework for teaching.* Alexandria, VA: ASCD.

Ainsworth, L. (2015). *"Unwrapping" the Common Core: A practical process to manage rigorous standards* (Leadership and Learning Center book). Boston: Houghton Mifflin Harcourt.

Baron-Cohen, S., & Wheelwright, S. (2004). The empathy quotient: An investigation of adults with Asperger syndrome or high functioning autism, and normal sex differences. *Journal of Autism and Developmental Disorders, 34*(2), 163–175.

Berwick, D. (1996). A primer to leading the improvement of systems. *BMJ, 312,* 619–622.

Couros, G. (2015). *The innovator's mindset: Empower learning, unleash talent, and lead a culture of creativity.* San Diego, CA: Dave Burgess Consulting.

Covey, S. R. (n.d.). Goodreads.com. Retrieved from http://www.goodreads.com/quotes/147819-we-judge-ourselves-by-our-intentions-and-others-by-their

Covey, S. R. (2004). *The 7 habits of highly effective people: Restoring the character ethic* (Rev. ed.). New York: Free Press.

Danielson, C. (2011) *The 2011 framework for teaching instrument.* Published electronically at https://www.danielsongroup.org/books-materials/

Danielson, C. (2015). Framing discussions about teaching. *Educational Leadership, 72*(7), 38–41.

Danielsongroup.org (n.d.). *The Framework.* Retrieved from https://www.danielsongroup.org/framework/

DuFour, R., DuFour, R., Eaker, R., & Many, T. (2010). *Learning by doing: A handbook for professional learning communities at work.* Bloomington, IN: Solution Tree Press.

Dynarski, M. (2016). *Teacher evaluations have been a waste of time and money.* Retrieved from https://www.brookings.edu/research/teacher-observations-have-been-a-waste-of-time-and-money/

Gallup. (2016). *Employee engagement* (Workplace engagement survey). Retrieved from www.gallup.com/topic/employee_engagement.aspx

Gardner, H. (1995). *Leading minds: An anatomy of leadership.* New York: Basic Books.

Gawande, A. (2010). *The checklist manifesto: How to get things right.* New York: Metropolitan Books.

Gladwell, M. (2005). *Blink: The power of thinking without thinking.* New York: Little Brown.

Hattie, J. (2012). *Visible learning for teachers: Maximizing impact on learning.* London: Routledge.

Jowett, B. (1892). Introduction. *The dialogues of Plato.* (B. Jowett Trans., 3rd ed., Vol. 3, pg. cci). Oxford University Press: London.

Lorenzanza, A. (n.d.). Goodreads. Retrieved from https://www.goodreads.com/author/quotes/4463656.Ashly_Lorenzana

Marzano, R. J., Frontier, T., & Livingston, D. (2011). *Effective supervision: Supporting the art and science of teaching.* Alexandria, VA: ASCD.

Marzano, R., & Toth, M. (2013). *Teacher evaluation that makes a difference: A new model for teacher growth and student achievement.* Alexandria, VA. ASCD.

McKinsey Report. (2007). *How the world's best-performing school systems come out on top.* Retrieved from http://alamin99.wordpress.com/2008/02/22/mckinsey-report/

Meyer, U., & Coffey, W. R. (2015). *Above the line: Lessons in leadership and life from a championship season.* New York: Penguin Press.

Nelson, E. C., Mohr, J. J., Batalden, P. B., Plume, S. K. (1996). Improving health care, part 1: The clinical value compass. *Joint Commission Journal on Quality Improvement, 22,* 243–258.

Senge, P. M. (1990). *The fifth discipline: The art and practice of the learning organization.* New York: Doubleday/Currency.

Sinek, S. (2010). How great leaders inspire action. [Video podcast]. Retrieved from https://www.ted.com/talks/simon_sinek_how_great_leaders_inspire_action

Sterner, T. (n.d.). Goodreads. Retrieved from https://www.goodreads.com/author/quotes/192606.Thomas_M_Sterner

Stiggins, R. J., Arter, J., Chappuis, J., & Chappuis, S. (2004). *Classroom assessment for student learning: Doing it right—Using it well.* Portland, OR: Assessment Training Institute.

Thoreau, H. D. (n.d). Goodreads. (Original quote from *Walden*, published 1854).

Valvano, J. (1993). ESPY Address in New York City. Retrieved from https://www.jimmyv.org/about/remembering-jim/espy-awards-speech/

Wiggins, G., & McTighe, J. (1998). *Understanding by design.* Alexandria, VA: Association for Supervision and Curriculum Development.

Index

CORWIN LEADERSHIP

Simon T. Bailey & Marceta F. Reilly
On providing a simple, sustainable framework that will help you move your school from mediocrity to brilliance.

Edie L. Holcomb
Use data to construct an equitable learning environment, develop instruction, and empower effective PL communities.

Debbie Silver & Dedra Stafford
Equip educators to develop resilient and mindful learners primed for academic growth and personal success.

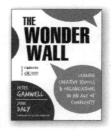

Peter Gamwell & Jane Daly
A fresh perspective on how to nurture creativity, innovation, leadership, and engagement.

Steven Katz, Lisa Ain Dack, & John Malloy
Leverage the oppositional forces of top-down expectations and bottom-up experience to create an intelligent, responsive school.

Lyn Sharratt & Beate Planche
A resource-rich guide that provides a strategic path to achieving sustainable communities of deep learners.

Peter M. DeWitt
Meet stakeholders where they are, motivate them to improve, and model how to do it.

Leadership that Makes an Impact

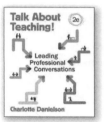

Charlotte Danielson
Harness the power of informal professional conversation and invite teachers to boost achievement.

Liz Wiseman, Lois Allen, & Elise Foster
Use leadership to bring out the best in others—liberating staff to excel and doubling your team's effectiveness.

Eric Sheninger
Use digital resources to create a new school culture, increase engagement, and facilitate real-time PD.

Russell J. Quaglia, Michael J. Corso, & Lisa L. Lande
Listen to your school's voice to see how you can increase engagement, involvement, and academic motivation.

Michael Fullan, Joanne Quinn, & Joanne McEachen
Learn the right drivers to mobilize complex, coherent, whole-system change and transform learning for all students.

CORWIN LEADERSHIP

A SAGE Publishing Company

Solutions you want. Experts you trust.
Results you need.

AUTHOR CONSULTING

Author Consulting
On-site professional learning with sustainable results! Let us help you design a professional learning plan to meet the unique needs of your school or district. www.corwin.com/pd

INSTITUTES

Institutes
Corwin Institutes provide collaborative learning experiences that equip your team with tools and action plans ready for immediate implementation. www.corwin.com/institutes

ECOURSES

eCourses
Practical, flexible online professional learning designed to let you go at your own pace. www.corwin.com/ecourses

READ2EARN

Read2Earn
Did you know you can earn graduate credit for reading this book? Find out how: www.corwin.com/read2earn

Contact an account manager at (800) 831-6640 or visit **www.corwin.com** for more information.